This guide is DEDICATED to all who love the countryside and enjoy exploring it; in GRATITUDE to all walkers who have helped in the creation and maintenance of THE WEALDWAY and to all authorities, landowners and others who have co-operated so helpfully.

WEALDWAY

	Page
Wealdway Introduction	2 & 3
Wealdway Tips	4
Wealdway Order Form & Comments Slip. Insert between	4 & 5
Accommodation & Public Transport	5
Weather: Shopping, Refreshments & Early Closing Days	6
Kit Check List: Strip Map Symbols	7
Gravesend Town Map: (Town to A2 Tollgate)	8
Gravesend (A2 Tollgate) to Luddesdown	9
Luddesdown to Trottiscliffe (NDW)	10
Trottiscliffe to Platt	11
Platt to West Peckham	12
West Peckham to Barnes Street	13
Barnes Street to Tonbridge	14 & 15
Tonbridge Town Map	14
Tonbridge to Modest Corner, Southborough	16
Modest Corner, Southborough to Stone Cross	17
Stone Cross to Withyham	18
Route Planner, Mileage Chart, Map & Diary. Between	18 & 19
Withyham to Top of Ashdown Forest	19
Top of Ashdown Forest to Browns Brook Cottage	20
Browns Brook Cottage to Buxted Park	21
Buxted Park to Blackboys	22
Uckfield Town Map: (WW route to Town)	23
Blackboys to East Hoathly	24
East Hoathly to Gun Hill	25
Gun Hill to A22 (Nr Hailsham)	26
A22 (Nr Hailsham) to Arlington	27
Arlington to Folkington (Link path to Berwick Sta.)	28
Long Man of Wilmington	29
Folkington to Eastbourne	30
Eastbourne Town Map (Link path to South Downs Way)	31
Ramblers' Association	32
The Ramblers' Association: Membership Form. Between	32 & 33
The Future of Wealdway & After Your Wealdway Walk	33
Connecting Long Distance Routes with Wealdway	34
Further Reading: Kent & Sussex	35
Useful Addresses: Country Code	36

Wealden Landscape

The information contained in this guide is believed to be correct at the time of publication. The Wealdway Committee, whilst accepting no responsibility for inaccuracies, will be pleased to receive details of any problem encountered on the route. A 'Comments' slip is provided between pages 4 and 5.

WEALDWAY INTRODUCTION

The Wealdway was originally conceived in the early 1970s by members of the Ramblers' Association as an attractive scenic route through the Weald of Kent and Sussex, also linking the North Downs Way to the South Downs Way. As the years have passed and new routes have appeared, it now links no less than seven major long distance paths. These are listed with details on page 34.

Although route descriptions of the Wealdway between Gravesend and Uckfield were published in the mid-seventies, it took nine years of intensive endeavour to complete the necessary ground-work and to produce a comprehensive guide. The final opening took place at Camp Hill on Ashdown Forest on 27 September 1981 when Mr. Derek Barber (now Sir), Chairman of the Countryside Commission, unveiled a commemorative plaque in the presence of representatives of seventeen member countries of the European Ramblers' Association and a huge gathering of 500 ramblers. Financial aid and enthusiasm for the concept also came from the Countryside Commission, the Sports Council, East Sussex County Council, Kent County Council, Wealden District Council, Tonbridge & Malling District Council, the South East England Tourist Board and last but not least, from the various ramblers groups, for without their hard work and inspiration, this major amenity would not have been created.

During the next nine years, many challenges had to be met head-on to protect the route from despoiling developments. Before the 1981 opening, the construction of the M20 motorway and the Tonbridge Flood Relief Barrier to name but two problems, had necessitated route changes. It was not to be long before new threats loomed to despoil other sections, ranging from oil rigs to an aerodrome.

In 1982 the Ministry of Defence purchased a sizeable chunk of land at Luddesdown, threatening to turn the lovely 'Bowling Alley' valley into an Army mine laying range. The RA, along with many other conservationist groups, joined battle to save the valley. After an agonizing year of doubt, the ministerial enquiry refused planning permission and the MoD had to sell the land, which is once again in private hands and so, for the present, this lovely valley is safeguarded.

That victory was soon overshadowed when proposals were made to exploit a considerable part of the Medway Valley for gravel extraction. This also was opposed by the

---

© Geoffrey King: Wealdway Committee – 1990
ISBN 0 9516006 0 5

Published by:
The Wealdway Committee: Ramblers' Association (Kent & Sussex Areas)
11 Old London Road, Brighton, E. Sussex BN1 8XR

Chairman	:	Dr. B. Perkins	Sussex Area
Secretary	:	Mr. M. Temple	Kent Area
Guide Design	:	Mr. G. King	Kent Area
Field Officer	:	Mr. V. Fowler	Kent Area
Field Officer	:	Mr. G. Mills	Sussex Area

1st Edition	:	1981
1st Edition	:	1982 (Reprint)
2nd Edition	:	1990 (Fully Revised)

Printed by Flo-Print, Langton Green,
Tunbridge Wells, Kent. Tel: (0892) 863388

All rights reserved. No part of this book may be reproduced or transmitted in any form or by any means, electronic or mechanical, including photocopying, recording or by any information storage retrieval system, without the permission of the publisher.

RA but permission was finally granted and now the first of several sites is being quarried near Tonbridge, right alongside the Wealdway. The WW Committee has been active in obtaining screening measures to mitigate the visual impact.

The 1985 RA Jubilee Walk around England followed 45 miles of Wealdway, from Barnes Street to Horsebridge. The Jubilee walkers arrived in Tonbridge on 9 April and were duly accommodated and entertained by local ramblers. The next day they joined a gathering of over two hundred ramblers, civic dignitaries and RA Chairman David Rubinstein, who unveiled the impressive Wealdway Route Sign, which stands on route at the entrance to the castle grounds. A one day Wealdway exhibition was also held in the castle.

The following year, on 23 August 1986, an astounding feat was performed when Kim Stanley, a member of the Tonbridge Athletic Club, ran the whole 80 miles of Wealdway from Gravesend to Eastbourne in fourteen hours, raising funds for Imperial Cancer Research.

On the night of 15 October 1987, almost without warning, a hurricane now commonly referred to as the 'Great Storm' swept across Southern England. In little more than a couple of hours, 15,000,000 trees crashed to the ground. Wealdway suffered its share of damage although the route was soon cleared. Signs of the havoc will remain for many years and some places may never look the same again. Several more storms with winds up to 100 mph caused further damage in early 1990.

Many walkers, especially those from distant parts, often express surprise at the variety of terrain and the feeling of remoteness on much of the route, in a region generally regarded as the overcrowded South East.

Undoubtedly, the Wealdway yields its charm in the myriad variation and intimate nature of its hills and valleys with sudden striking views and enchanting woodland and meadows.

Most Wealdway walkers, refreshed in mind and spirit, finish their walk having delighted in the pleasures of the route and its surrounding countryside. Often they continue on the South Downs Way or along other linking long distance paths.

Whichever direction you take, we hope you enjoy Wealdway and use of this guide. Our best wishes go with you.

View of the South Downs from Wealdway at Crest Cottage near Camp Hill

WEALDWAY TIPS

Using the guide in navigation and getting the most enjoyment from your walk.

This guide keeps written description to the minimum using only 'back-up' explanation where difficult places may cause doubt. Guide navigation is based on the continuous strip map principle, each mile is marked as you progress. The route is slightly repeated at the top and bottom as you turn from page to page.

The information and strip map is limited to appropriate details for simple and effective use. Firstly, familiarise yourself with the symbols on page seven then, reading from the strip maps, look for the corresponding landmarks denoted by the symbols and you'll know your whereabouts at all times.

Other maps are not strictly necessary but in plotting the route from this guide into the context of surrounding countryside, they will be essential, especially in pre-planning a walk of several days duration. The maps needed will be a worthwhile investment and Ordnance Survey Maps on at least the 1:50,000 scale will be best suited to your purpose. You will need four 'Landranger' sheets Nos. 177, 188, 198 and 199. These cover the entire route and you will find Wealdway featured on them. They will also be useful for excursions off-route.

The Wealdway generally provides non-strenuous walking across fairly easy terrain, but this depends on daily mileage attempted and the prevailing weather conditions. Ashdown Forest can be bleak in winter and Wealden clay in places can be slippery but it is often a matter of luck and observance of weather forecasts. A winter's day walk can often be a most glorious and unforgettable experience.

The route is never far from civilisation and should be suitable even for the occasional rambler, since it can be tackled in modest stages, without elaborate walking gear. However you will need some basic kit and to assist in selecting this, a 'Kit Check List' is provided on page seven, with several columns to tick should your party be numerous. Light boots are by far the best but whatever footwear you use, make sure it is 'worn-in' and that it has adequate tread. Don't leave your waterproofs behind to scimp on weight, nothing is more miserable than to be caught out in an unexpected storm.

It is important for your rucksack to be comfortable and can hold the items you wish to carry. Avoid satchels with one shoulder strap as they do not distribute weight evenly, can cause aches and can swing, thereby throwing you off balance in an awkward place, e.g. when crossing a stile. Try also to avoid mini rucksacks. They may look light and small but they too can cause aches because the carrying straps rely entirely on your shoulders. A good rucksack, properly fitted to your hips, will carry a reasonable weight in comfort without one being aware of it.

If you have never walked long distances before, either by the day or by longer periods, try to start with a low mileage and work up to a higher mileage after a few days. Ten to twelve miles a day is average, allowing for an unhurried pace of two to three miles per hour. If you are out for a week or longer, allow for the occasional rest day which can also be used for the deviating excursion to nearby places of interest.

Finally, don't forget to leave a note with your friends/relatives about where you expect to be, especially if you intend walking alone.

Have fun.

River Medway

Royal Oak, Hayesden

WEALDWAY ORDER FORM

	Each	Quantity	£ . p
WEALDWAY GUIDE (A gift for a friend/relative) :	£3.50		
ACCOMMODATION LIST (See page 5) :	£1.00		
EMBROIDERED BADGE (See inside Front Cover photo) :	£1.40		

The above prices are subject to change after the year of publication of this guide

TOTAL :

BLOCK LETTERS PLEASE

NAME: Mr. Mrs. Miss Ms.
ADDRESS

COUNTY   POST CODE

P&P inclusive
Please make chqs/POs payable to
SUSSEX AREA RAMBLERS' ASSOCIATION

Place this order form into a stamped envelope and address as over

---

WEALDWAY COMMENTS

If you encounter a particular problem on Wealdway, or wish to mention a point of interest about the route or guide, perhaps to tell us about new accommodation you have found, we shall be pleased to receive this slip.

NOTE: For a number of reasons it is regretted we cannot accept comments for changes in route. Most alternatives have been fully reviewed and it is felt any deviations are best left for the individual walker to explore.

Please complete the form, then place it in a stamped envelope addressed to
RA (SUSSEX AREA) · 11 OLD LONDON ROAD · BRIGHTON · E. SUSSEX · BN1 8XR

COMMENTS	STRIP MAP PAGE No:	MAP REF:

Please continue overleaf

WEALDWAY ORDER FORM

Please complete your requirements overleaf, then place this form in an envelope and send it to the address shown below. If you wish to make an enquiry only, please send a stamped addressed envelope.

⇨ RAMBLERS' ASSOCIATION SUSSEX AREA
11 OLD LONDON ROAD
BRIGHTON
EAST SUSSEX
BN1 8XR

⇩ Please ensure you have signed your cheque and stamped the envelope.

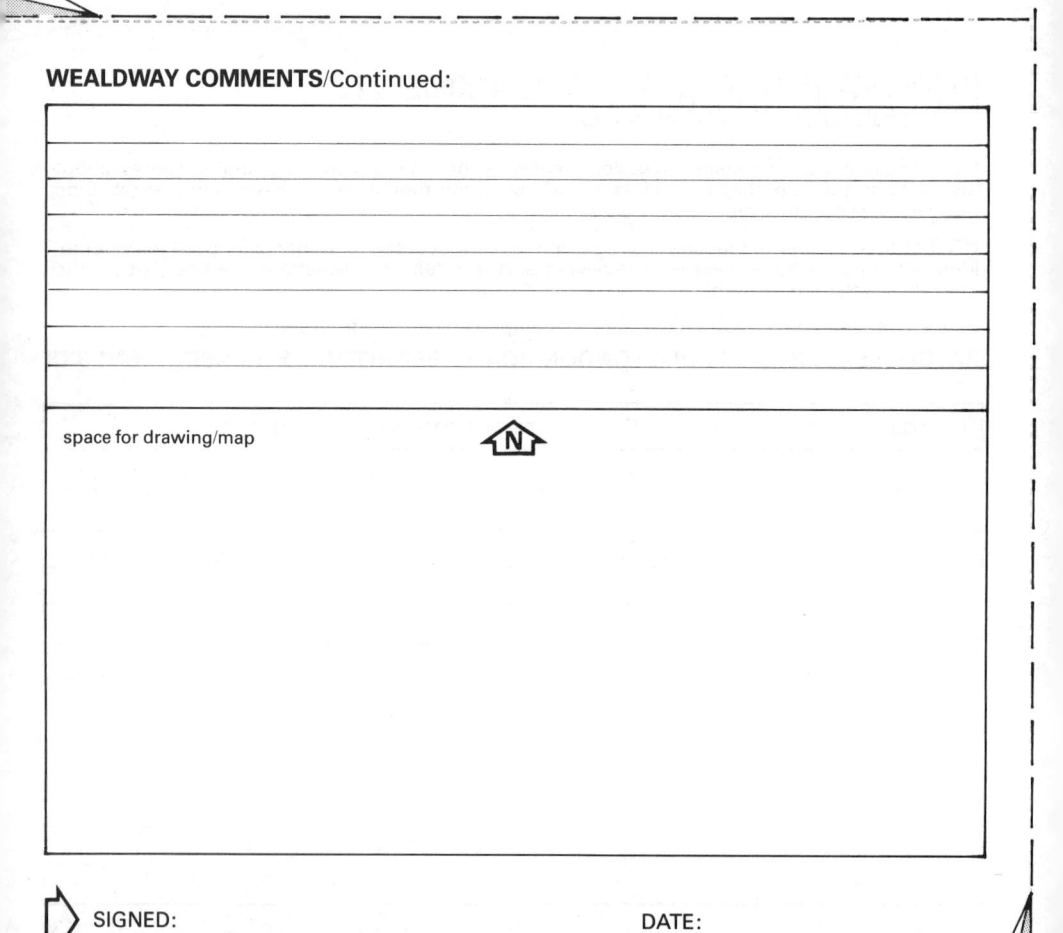

WEALDWAY COMMENTS/Continued:

space for drawing/map   N

SIGNED: _____   DATE: _____

ACCOMMODATION ON WEALDWAY

For those walkers who prefer a continuous walk, i.e. in daily stages, Wealdway now has a variety of accommodation, either on or near the route, throughout its length in the two counties.

A constantly up-dated Accommodation List is produced bi-annually by the Wealdway Committee. At a modest charge – post free – a copy can be obtained by completing the Order Form opposite this page. From this list you should be able to choose addresses suited to the daily distances planned. To assist in forward planning, a Route Planner section is provided between pages 18-19. From this, unfamiliar places can be identified in name, in mileage and in relationship to the strip maps as well as the route as a whole.

In summer months, it is recommended that accommodation should be booked in advance and it is strongly advised not to turn up speculatively as accommodation in the remoter areas, apart from the List addresses, may be hard to find unless you are prepared to travel considerable distances from the route.

Further information about accommodation in the Wealdway area may be obtained from the South East England Tourist Board, see page 36.

CAMPING

There are no known camp sites on or near the Wealdway. Camping may be possible if permission can be obtained from farmers landowners, etc.

PUBLIC TRANSPORT INFORMATION

Bus services

Excellent information can be obtained from the following sources:

Kent
Public Transport Group
Kent County Council
Springfield
Maidstone
Kent ME14 2LX
Tel: (0622) 696943

East Sussex
Rider Services
c/o County Engineer
East Sussex County Council
Phoenix Causeway
Lewes, East Sussex BN7 1UE
Tel: (0273) 478007 or 482123

Bridge near Withyham

In recent years there have been many changes to the local bus services, the range of companies and routes now being so numerous that it is impossible to list them comprehensively here in this guide.

British Rail Services

Page	Route Place	Nearest BR Station	Proximity/Miles to Wealdway
8	Gravesend	Gravesend	¼ (Town Pier)
9	A2 Tollgate	Gravesend	2 (see Gravesend Town Map)
11 & 12	Platt	Borough Green	1
14 & 15	Tonbridge	Tonbridge	½
16 & 17	Modest Corner	Tunbridge Wells	2½ (Bus service to Southboro')
17 & 18	Stone Cross	Ashurst	1¼
18	Stone Cross	Ashurst	1 (FP to WW at 513 379)
21 & 22	Buxted Park	Buxted	¾
23	Hempstead Mill	Uckfield	1 (Lane to WW at 483 218)
28	Arlington	Berwick	1 (FP from route 536 068)
31	Eastbourne	Eastbourne	1¾ (from end/start of WW)

It may be difficult to obtain service information at some of the above stations. Passenger service enquiries for these stations and Network South East can be best obtained from all BR telephone enquiry bureaux.

LONDON: 071 928 5100 Open continuously
TONBRIDGE: (0732) 770111 Mon to Sat: 07.15 to 21.45
  Sun: 08.15 to 21.45
BRIGHTON: (0273) 206755 Mon to Sat: 07.15 to 21.15
  Sun: 08.15 to 21.45

WEATHER

Weather in the South East corner of England can be as erratic as in most parts of Britain, but in general there is more sun and warmer temperatures than elsewhere.

The two better periods for walking the Wealdway are the Spring and Autumn. In the Spring the countryside acquires a new freshness with flowers and trees breaking into bud, with the pastel shades of blossom gracing late April and early May. The glorious colours of Autumn are usually in mid October and early November.

In the summer months, June to September, some days can be very hot with views obscured by heat haze. The winter months change the landscape, frost and snow adding a new dimension. A day's walk must allow for the shorter winter day and possible heavy going on muddy paths. In a severe winter, snow can be quite deep but most winters are snow free.

Sea mists can roll inland for a few miles, even when the Weald is enjoying fine weather, but this phenomenon is infrequent. The weather can also vary from coast to coast, north or south; if still in doubt after listening to radio forecasts, you can check with the following:

MET. OFFICE WEATHER INFORMATION
Available 24 hours, 7 days a week.
Updated 3 or more times per day.
CHARGES: Incl. VAT (Subject to change)
25p per minute   cheap rate
38p per minute   at all other times
5 DAY: NATIONAL Forecast 0898 500 430
METEOROLOGICAL OFFICE: DIAL 0898 500 402 ▶ DAILY: NATIONAL Forecast

SHOPPING · REFRESHMENTS · EARLY CLOSING DAYS

It is appreciated that walkers are mainly interested in purchases of food for packed lunches etc. Unfortunately, there are only a few village shops left along the route. These are listed on the strip maps but they may not remain open in future years. So if you intend buying food and drink, be sure you do so before setting out on a section which may not be served by a shop. The large towns will be no problem as many food shops, cafes, etc. remain open even on early closing day, which is Wednesday for Gravesend, Tonbridge, Tunbridge Wells, Uckfield, Hailsham and Eastbourne.

All the public houses on or very near the Wealdway are indicated on the strip maps. All vary their opening hours but at most, food and bar meals are available at lunch time and in the evenings, seven days a week.

▲ Looking south, Nash Street (p.9)

WEALDWAY
KIT CHECK LIST

Members of party
✓ ✓ ✓ ✓

STRIP MAP SYMBOLS

	Strong shoes with good treads. Preferably boots.
	Comfortable rucksack to fit snugly on waist.
	Waterproof jacket with hood or hat and over-trousers.
	Food and drink enough for a day out.
	This guide. Any maps you wish to take. Time table.
	Camera. Spare film. Binoculars. Pocket knife.
	Simple first-aid. Plasters. Pain-killers.
	Watch. Wallet. Purse. Cash. Pen/Pencil.
	Perhaps a spare sweater if very cold.
	For winter walking. A hat and gloves. Scarf.
	Handkerchief. Comb. Make-up. Reading/Sun glasses.
	A note left of your whereabouts.

Symbol	Meaning
7	Page / Map No
	Main Route
	Deviating Footpath
(10)	Mileage Point
(048 325)	Map Reference
	Road or Lane
	Track or Driveway
	Fence, Hedge or Wall
	Stile/Gate
	Buildings
+ ✝ ✝	Churches
	River
	Stream
	Railway/Station
	Bridge
	Power Line
	Embankment
	Woodland/Forest
	Heath/Parkland
	Scrub
	Rocks
	Pond/Lake
	View Point
425 ft	Height above Sea Level
P.O.	Post Office
C.P.	Car Park
S.P.	Sign Post
N.T.	National Trust

SCALE of STRIP MAPS: 2½" per mile
(1:25,000)

O.S. MAPS if needed : Scale 50,000
Nos: : 177, 188, 198, 199
O.S. Maps 25,000 scale: Old & New Series numbers are also listed on each map page.

The Strip Maps are based upon the Ordnance Survey Map with the permission of the Controller of H.M. Stationery Office. Crown Copyright Reserved.

8 GRAVESEND TOWN MAP

GRAVESEND, river port set amid the marshlands of the lower Thames, affords fascinating views of the busy, colourful scene on this London artery. In the town centre some fine 19th Century buildings jostle more modern development. Southwards, where the urban area spreads towards farmlands & orchards, a sweeping panorama of the Kent & Essex banks of the river is seen from Windmill Hill.

Pier at Gravesend — G.K.

The start of Wealdway

Walkers who prefer to begin their journey in open country, can start the Wealdway at the 'Tollgate' Europa Hotel, situated on the south side of the A2. Claimants to a complete walk from waters edge to waters edge, (Thames to Channel), can start at the Town Pier & follow the largely urban & metalled route as shown on the Town map.

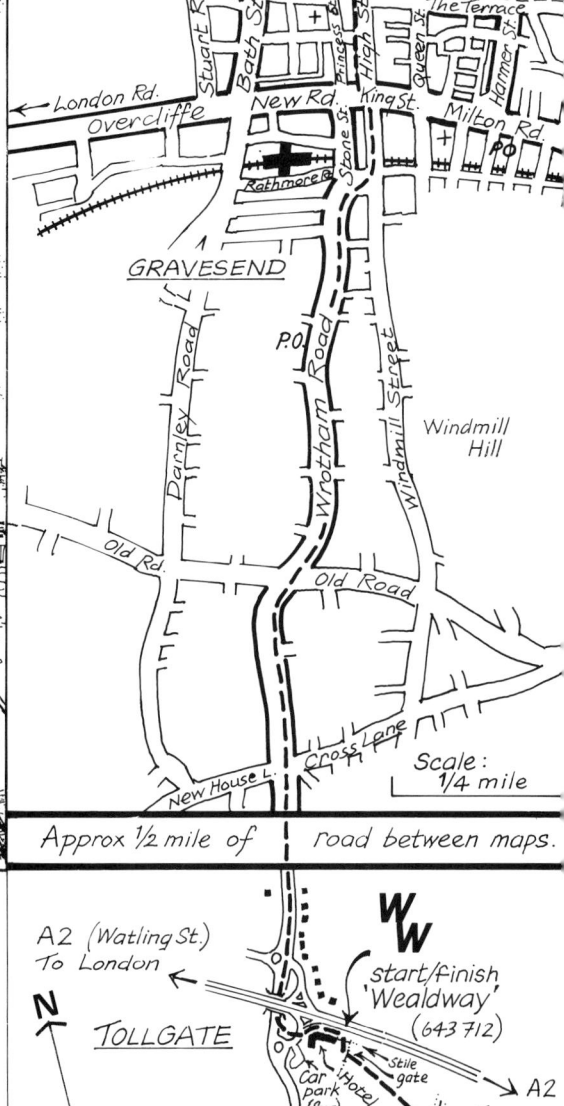

Scale: 1/4 mile

Approx 1/2 mile of road between maps.

A2 (Watling St.) To London

TOLLGATE

A227 To Tonbridge

start/finish 'Wealdway' (643 712)

A2 To Rochester

GRAVESEND (A2 TOLLGATE) TO LUDDESDOWN 9

Map annotations (clockwise from top left):

- TOLLGATE (643 713)
- Hotel, Car park (free), stile & gate, A2
- see p.6 "Start of Wealdway" (or the finish?)
- orchard
- unfenced metalled track
- Cottage
- playing field
- slightly staggered cross tracks
- 3 power lines
- 210 ft.
- (645 697)
- ①
- L.CW The London Countryway follows the same route from Gravesend to Sole Street
- To A227
- NASH STREET
- stiles ②
- (642 687)
- stiles
- stile
- A227 To Meopham Green
- stile by gate
- ③
- N.T. 'Yeomans House' (Open by appointment)
- shop
- B.R. Sta.
- 'The Railway Inn'
- L.CW
- SOLE STREET
- B2009
- white gate
- Camer Country Park
- Cottage
- L.CW
- (665 667) stiles
- ④
- L.CW
- "Golden Lion P.H."
- 360 ft. steep slope
- wire fence
- Stiles
- Stile & steps
- LUDDESDOWN

GK

As soon as one leaves the A2, it is quiet & remote, though flat & unremarkable. Starting thus, through intensively farmed countryside, contrasts completely with the areas only a few miles ahead.

At the time of publication of this guide, the route & nature of the Channel Tunnel Rail Link is unknown. We can only speculate that the Wealdway will cross the Rail Link somewhere north of Nash Street?

MAPS O.S. 1:50,000 - 177
       1:25,000 - TQ 67/77 (1177)
                 TQ 66/76 (1193)

In <u>Sole Street</u> is a beautiful Tudor high-halled yeoman's dwelling, preserved by the National Trust. About one mile north-east, is the charming village of <u>Cobham</u> and its famous 'Leather Bottle' Inn, which Dickens featured in Pickwick Papers. Another N.T. property is 'Owletts', a fine red bricked house of the Restoration period.

The church at <u>Luddesdown</u> is much restored but attractively set, adjacent to a magnificent manor house 'Luddesdown Court', which may date back to 1100 or earlier. (Unfortunately it is not open to the public).

10 LUDDESDOWN TO TROTTISCLIFFE (North Downs Way)

An undulating section which climbs onto a chalk downland and follows the side of a beautiful, partially wooded valley south of Luddesdown. Several of the paths crossing open fields may be ploughed out and require careful navigation.

The modern "Battle of Luddesdown" Circa 1983
(see 'Introduction' on p.2)

G.K.

A feature of this section, is the magnificent sweep of The Bowling Alley, a valley about 1 mile long which is crossed diagonally. This view, looks north to the spur just south of Luddesdown.
Turning to the south, is the view of the attractive hamlet of Great Buckland.

G.K.

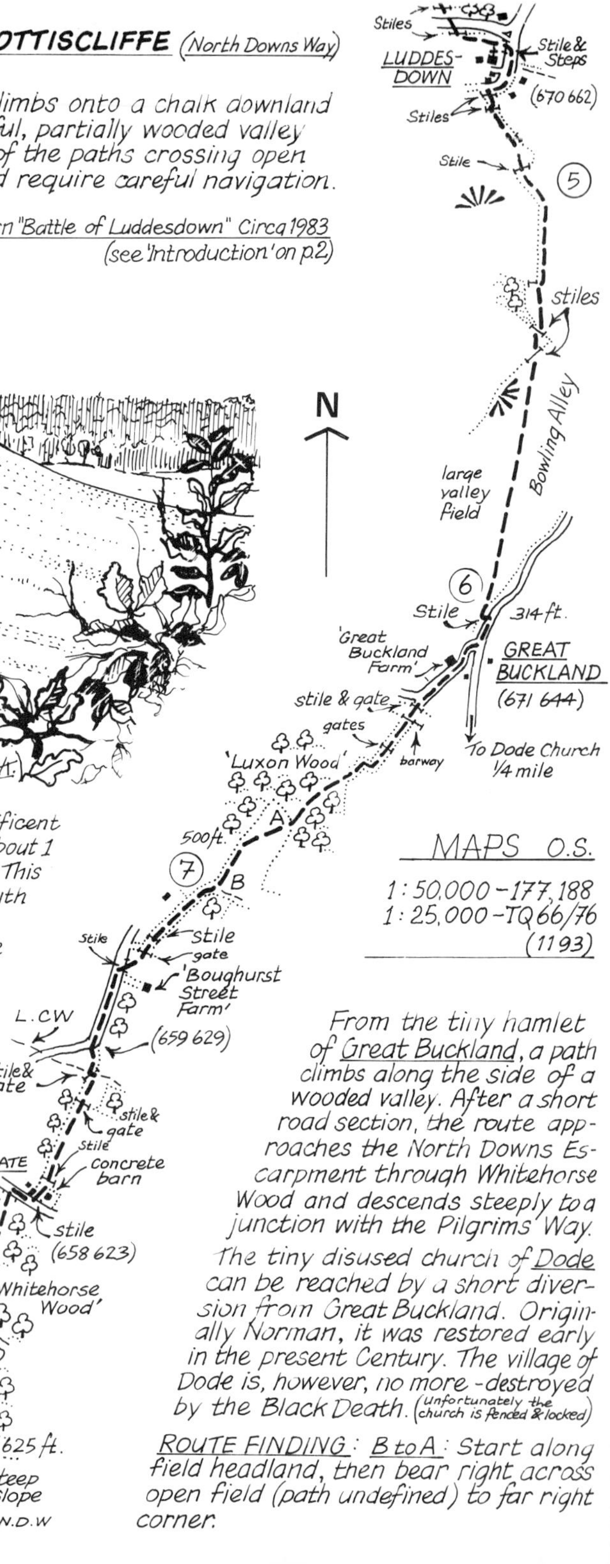
Stiles
LUDDES-DOWN
Stile & Steps
(670 662)
Stiles
Stile
5
stiles
Bowling Alley
N
large valley field
6
Stile
314 ft.
'Great Buckland Farm'
GREAT BUCKLAND
(671 644)
stile & gate
gates
barway
To Dode Church 1/4 mile
'Luxon Wood'
A
500 ft.
7
B
Stile
stile
gate
'Boughurst Street Farm'
L.CW
(659 629)
stile & gate
stile & gate
Stile
concrete barn
POUNDGATE
stile
stile
(658 623)
8
'Whitehorse Wood'
625 ft.
North Downs Way
Steps
steep slope
To Trottiscliffe
N.D.W
400 ft.

MAPS O.S.

1 : 50,000 – 177, 188
1 : 25,000 – TQ 66/76
(1193)

From the tiny hamlet of Great Buckland, a path climbs along the side of a wooded valley. After a short road section, the route approaches the North Downs Escarpment through Whitehorse Wood and descends steeply to a junction with the Pilgrims' Way.

The tiny disused church of Dode can be reached by a short diversion from Great Buckland. Originally Norman, it was restored early in the present Century. The village of Dode is, however, no more - destroyed by the Black Death. (Unfortunately the church is fenced & locked)

ROUTE FINDING: B to A: Start along field headland, then bear right across open field (path undefined) to far right corner.

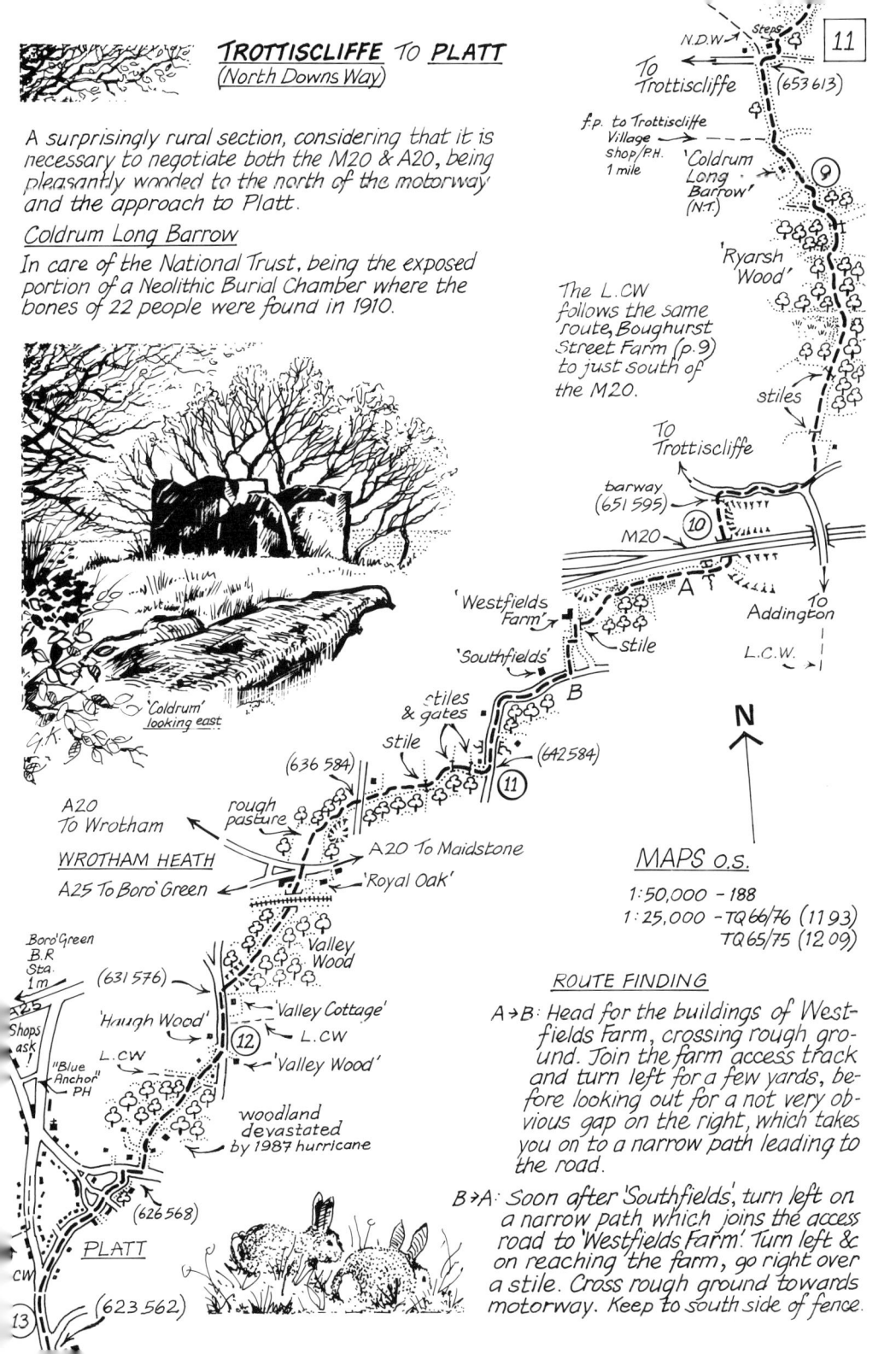

TROTTISCLIFFE TO PLATT
(North Downs Way)

A surprisingly rural section, considering that it is necessary to negotiate both the M20 & A20, being pleasantly wooded to the north of the motorway and the approach to Platt.

Coldrum Long Barrow

In care of the National Trust, being the exposed portion of a Neolithic Burial Chamber where the bones of 22 people were found in 1910.

'Coldrum' looking east

N.D.W. Steps
To Trottiscliffe (653 613)
f.p. to Trottiscliffe Village shop/P.H. 1 mile
'Coldrum Long Barrow' (N.T.)
'Ryarsh Wood'
stiles
To Trottiscliffe

The L.C.W follows the same route, Boughurst Street Farm (p.9) to just south of the M20.

barway (651 595)
M20
To Addington
L.C.W.
'Westfields Farm'
stile
'Southfields'
stiles & gates
stile
(636 584)
(642 584)
⑪

A20 To Wrotham
rough pasture
WROTHAM HEATH
A25 To Boro' Green
A20 To Maidstone
'Royal Oak'

Boro' Green B.R. Sta. 1m
Shops ask!
"Blue Anchor" P.H.
(631 576)
'Hough Wood'
L.C.W
Valley Wood
'Valley Cottage'
L.C.W
⑫
'Valley Wood'
woodland devastated by 1987 hurricane

(626 568)
PLATT
(623 562)

MAPS O.S.
1:50,000 - 188
1:25,000 - TQ 66/76 (11 93)
TQ 65/75 (12 09)

ROUTE FINDING

A→B: Head for the buildings of Westfields Farm, crossing rough ground. Join the farm access track and turn left for a few yards, before looking out for a not very obvious gap on the right, which takes you on to a narrow path leading to the road.

B→A: Soon after 'Southfields', turn left on a narrow path which joins the access road to 'Westfields Farm'. Turn left & on reaching the farm, go right over a stile. Cross rough ground towards motorway. Keep to south side of fence.

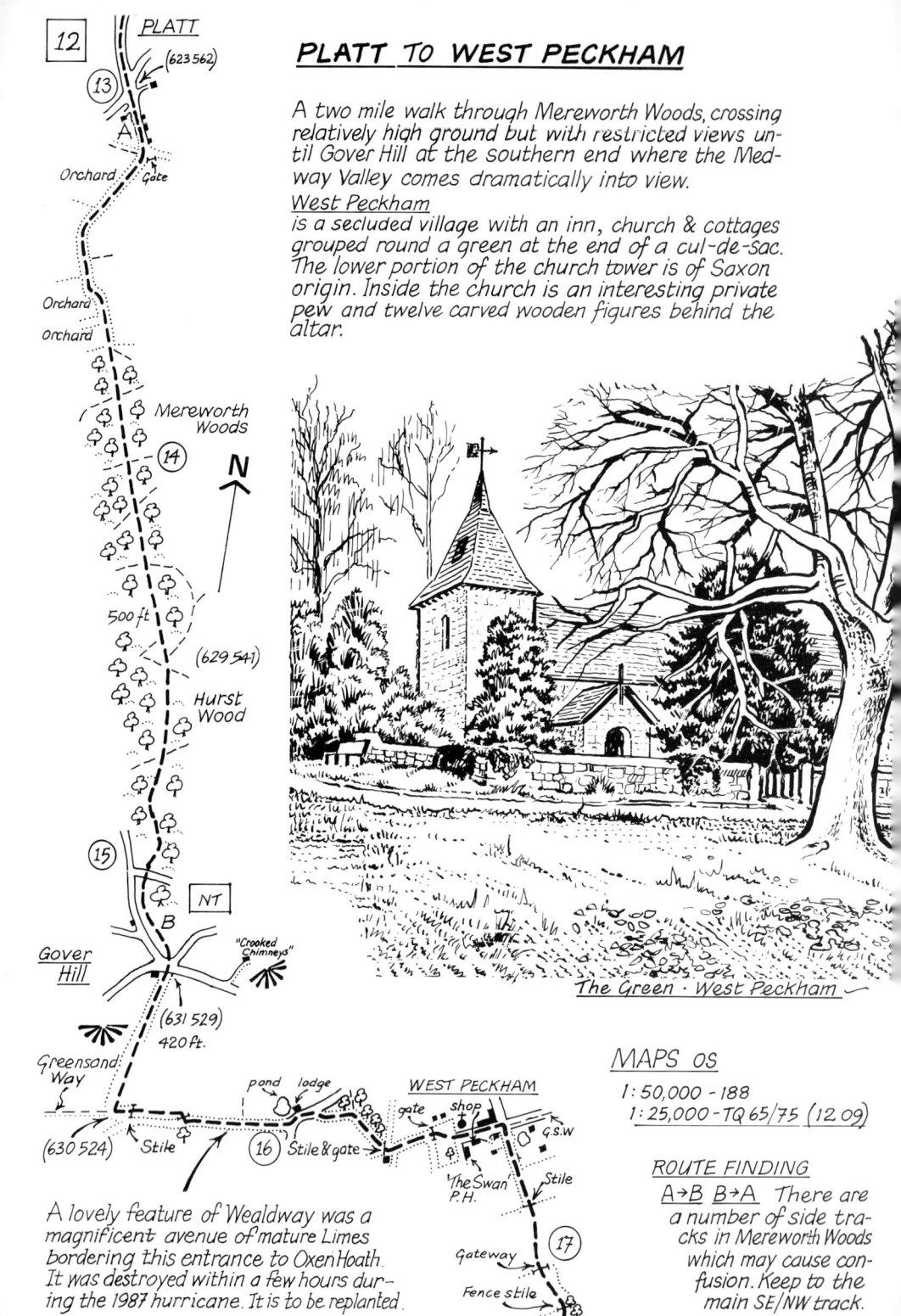

PLATT TO WEST PECKHAM

A two mile walk through Mereworth Woods, crossing relatively high ground but with restricted views until Gover Hill at the southern end where the Medway Valley comes dramatically into view.

West Peckham
is a secluded village with an inn, church & cottages grouped round a green at the end of a cul-de-sac. The lower portion of the church tower is of Saxon origin. Inside the church is an interesting private pew and twelve carved wooden figures behind the altar.

The Green · West Peckham

MAPS OS
1:50,000 - 188
1:25,000 - TQ 65/75 (12 09)

ROUTE FINDING
A→B B→A There are a number of side tracks in Mereworth Woods which may cause confusion. Keep to the main SE/NW track.

A lovely feature of Wealdway was a magnificent avenue of mature Limes bordering this entrance to Oxen Hoath. It was destroyed within a few hours during the 1987 hurricane. It is to be replanted.

WEST PECKHAM TO BARNES STREET | 13

An easy walk across the Medway Valley in a landscape which provides a typically Kentish blend of converted oast houses and orchards. There are several fine old buildings grouped round the road crossing at Barnes Street.

ROUTE FINDING
A→B B→A is likely to be ploughed & obstructed by plantings & fencing.

MAPS OS
1:50,000 – 188
1:25,000 – TQ 65/75 (12.09)
TQ 64/74 (12.29)

WEST PECKHAM
G.S.W.
Stile
'The Swan' P.H.
17
Gateway
Fencestile
stile
stile
stiles (653 514)
gate
isolated trees
derelict cottage
A26 To Tonbridge
Proposed diversion
18
N
gate at each bridge
sheds
'Peckham Place Farm'
(659 503)
Gate & stile
'Crowhurst Farm'
Orchards
footbridge
19
open field
track undefined
Kent Hse
(653 492)
B   A
very narrow lane
alternative path
stile
20
(649 485)
footbridge
foot-bridges
'Poplar Court'
gateway
stiles
BARNES STREET
21

G.K.

PUBLIC FOOTPATH

G.K.

14 | BARNES STREET TO TONBRIDGE & TONBRIDGE TOWN MAP

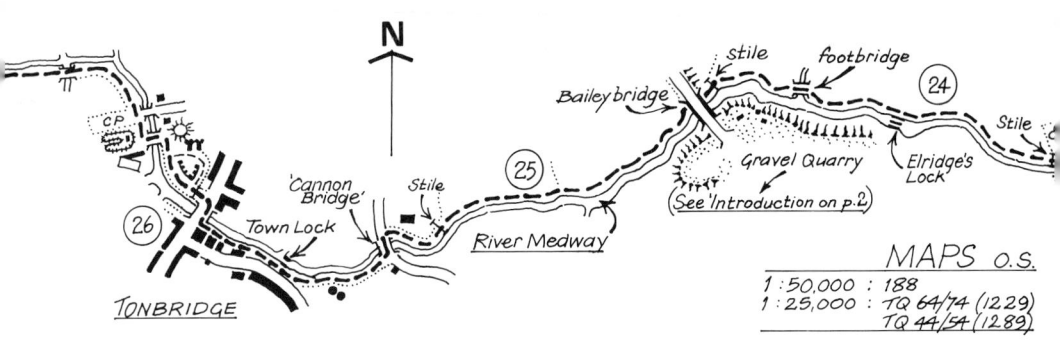

MAPS O.S.
1:50,000 : 188
1:25,000 : TQ 64/74 (12.29)
TQ 44/54 (12.89)

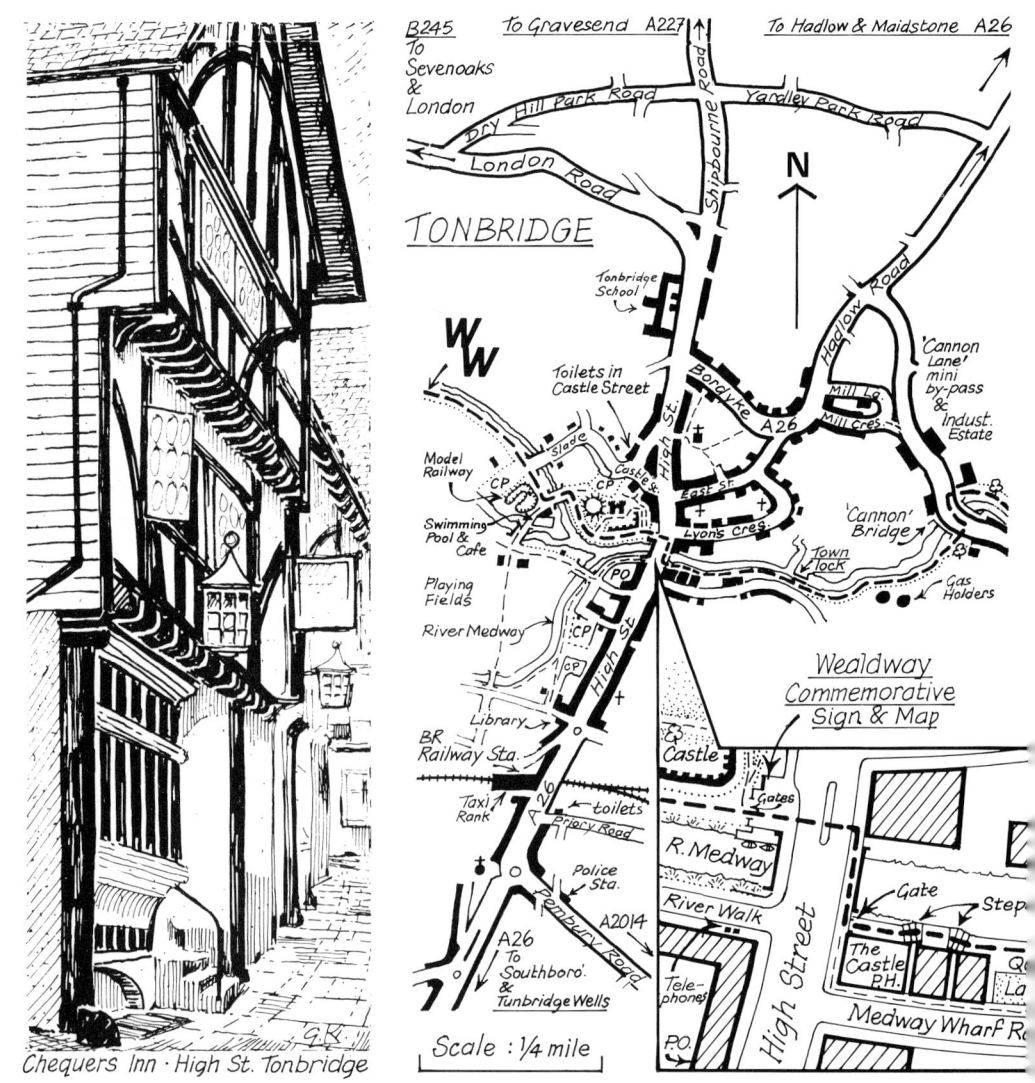

Labels on upper map: Bailey bridge, stile, footbridge, 24, Stile, Gravel Quarry, Elridge's Lock, See 'Introduction on p.2', 25, River Medway, Stile, 'Cannon Bridge', Town Lock, 26, TONBRIDGE, CP

Labels on Tonbridge town map:
B245 To Sevenoaks & London
To Gravesend A227
To Hadlow & Maidstone A26
Dry Hill Park Road, Shipbourne Road, Yardley Park Road
London Road
TONBRIDGE
Tonbridge School
WW
Toilets in Castle Street
Bordyke
Hadlow Road
'Cannon Lane' mini by-pass & Indust. Estate
Mill La, Mill Cres, A26
Model Railway
Slade, CP, Castle St, East St
CP, High St
'Cannon' Bridge
Swimming Pool & Cafe
Lyons Cres
Town lock
P.O.
Gas Holders
Playing Fields
River Medway
CP
CP
Library
BR Railway Sta.
Taxi Rank
toilets
Priory Road
Police Sta.
A26 To Southboro' & Tunbridge Wells
A2014 Pembury Road
Scale : 1/4 mile

Wealdway Commemorative Sign & Map
Castle
Gates
R. Medway
River Walk
Gate — Step
The Castle P.H.
High Street
Telephones
P.O.
Medway Wharf Rd

Chequers Inn · High St. Tonbridge

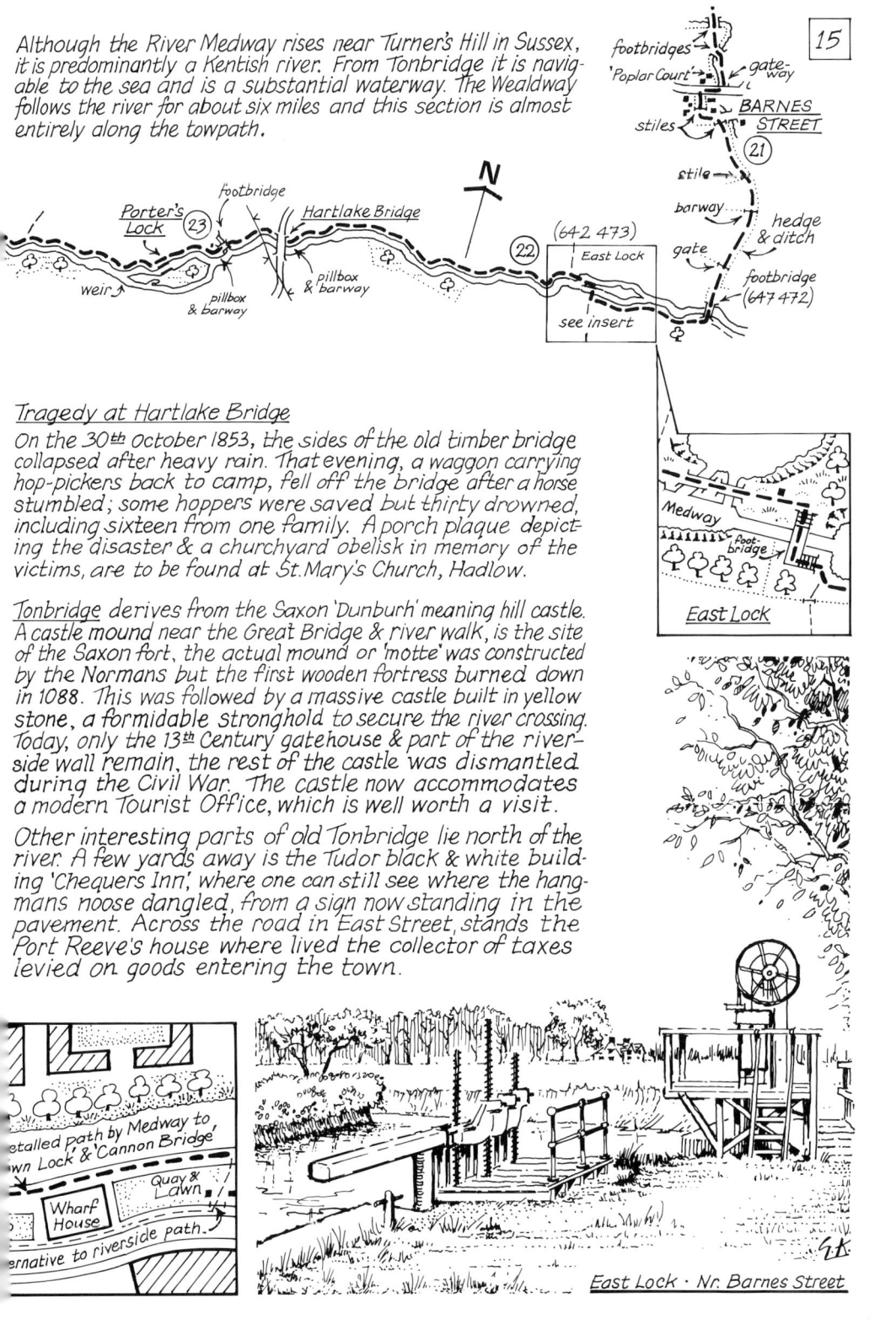

Although the River Medway rises near Turner's Hill in Sussex, it is predominantly a Kentish river. From Tonbridge it is navigable to the sea and is a substantial waterway. The Wealdway follows the river for about six miles and this section is almost entirely along the towpath.

Tragedy at Hartlake Bridge

On the 30th October 1853, the sides of the old timber bridge collapsed after heavy rain. That evening, a waggon carrying hop-pickers back to camp, fell off the bridge after a horse stumbled; some hoppers were saved but thirty drowned, including sixteen from one family. A porch plaque depicting the disaster & a churchyard obelisk in memory of the victims, are to be found at St. Mary's Church, Hadlow.

Tonbridge derives from the Saxon 'Dunburh' meaning hill castle. A castle mound near the Great Bridge & river walk, is the site of the Saxon fort, the actual mound or 'motte' was constructed by the Normans but the first wooden fortress burned down in 1088. This was followed by a massive castle built in yellow stone, a formidable stronghold to secure the river crossing. Today, only the 13th Century gatehouse & part of the riverside wall remain, the rest of the castle was dismantled during the Civil War. The castle now accommodates a modern Tourist Office, which is well worth a visit.

Other interesting parts of old Tonbridge lie north of the river. A few yards away is the Tudor black & white building 'Chequers Inn', where one can still see where the hangmans noose dangled, from a sign now standing in the pavement. Across the road in East Street, stands the Port Reeve's house where lived the collector of taxes levied on goods entering the town.

16 TONBRIDGE TO MODEST CORNER SOUTHBOROUGH

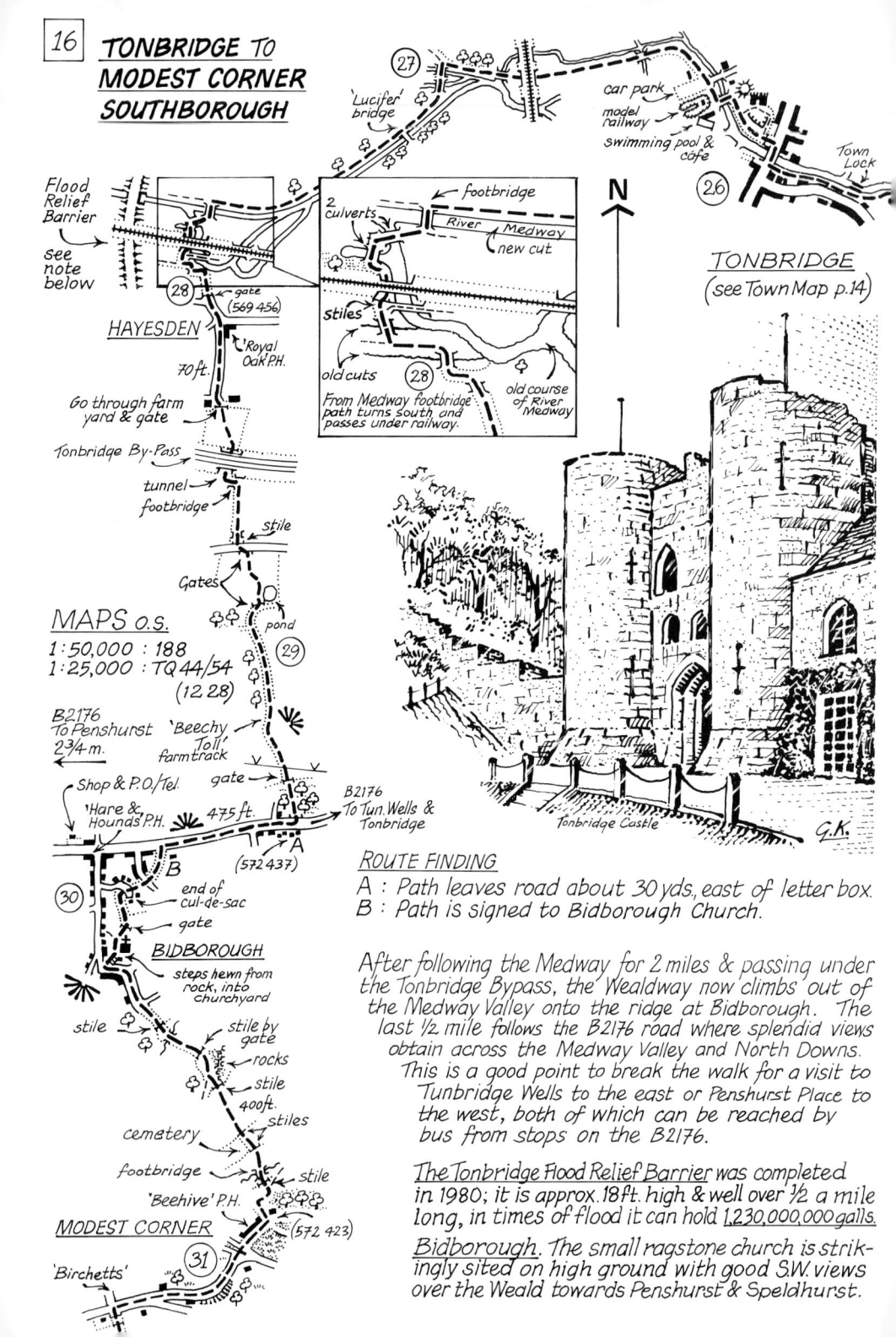

Lucifer bridge — 27

car park
model railway
swimming pool & café
Town Lock
26

Flood Relief Barrier
see note below

2 culverts — footbridge
River Medway
new cut

TONBRIDGE (see Town Map p.14)

28 gate (569 456)

HAYESDEN
70 ft.
'Royal Oak P.H.'
Go through farm yard & gate
Tonbridge By-Pass
tunnel footbridge
stile
Gates
pond
29

stiles
old cuts
From Medway footbridge path turns south and passes under railway.
old course of River Medway

MAPS O.S.
1:50,000 : 188
1:25,000 : TQ 44/54
(12.28)

B2176 To Penshurst 2¾ m.
'Beechy Toll' farm track
gate
Shop & P.O./Tel.
'Hare & Hounds' P.H.
475 ft.
B2176 To Tun. Wells & Tonbridge
A
(572 437)
B
30
end of cul-de-sac
gate
BIDBOROUGH
steps hewn from rock, into churchyard
stile
stile by gate
rocks
stile
400ft
stiles
cemetery
footbridge
stile
'Beehive' P.H.
MODEST CORNER
(572 423)
'Birchetts'
31

Tonbridge Castle — G.K.

ROUTE FINDING
A : Path leaves road about 30 yds. east of letter box.
B : Path is signed to Bidborough Church.

After following the Medway for 2 miles & passing under the Tonbridge Bypass, the Wealdway now climbs out of the Medway Valley onto the ridge at Bidborough. The last ½ mile follows the B2176 road where splendid views obtain across the Medway Valley and North Downs.
This is a good point to break the walk for a visit to Tunbridge Wells to the east or Penshurst Place to the west, both of which can be reached by bus from stops on the B2176.

<u>The Tonbridge Flood Relief Barrier</u> was completed in 1980; it is approx. 18 ft. high & well over ½ a mile long, in times of flood it can hold <u>1,230,000,000 galls</u>.

<u>Bidborough</u>. The small ragstone church is strikingly sited on high ground with good S.W. views over the Weald towards Penshurst & Speldhurst.

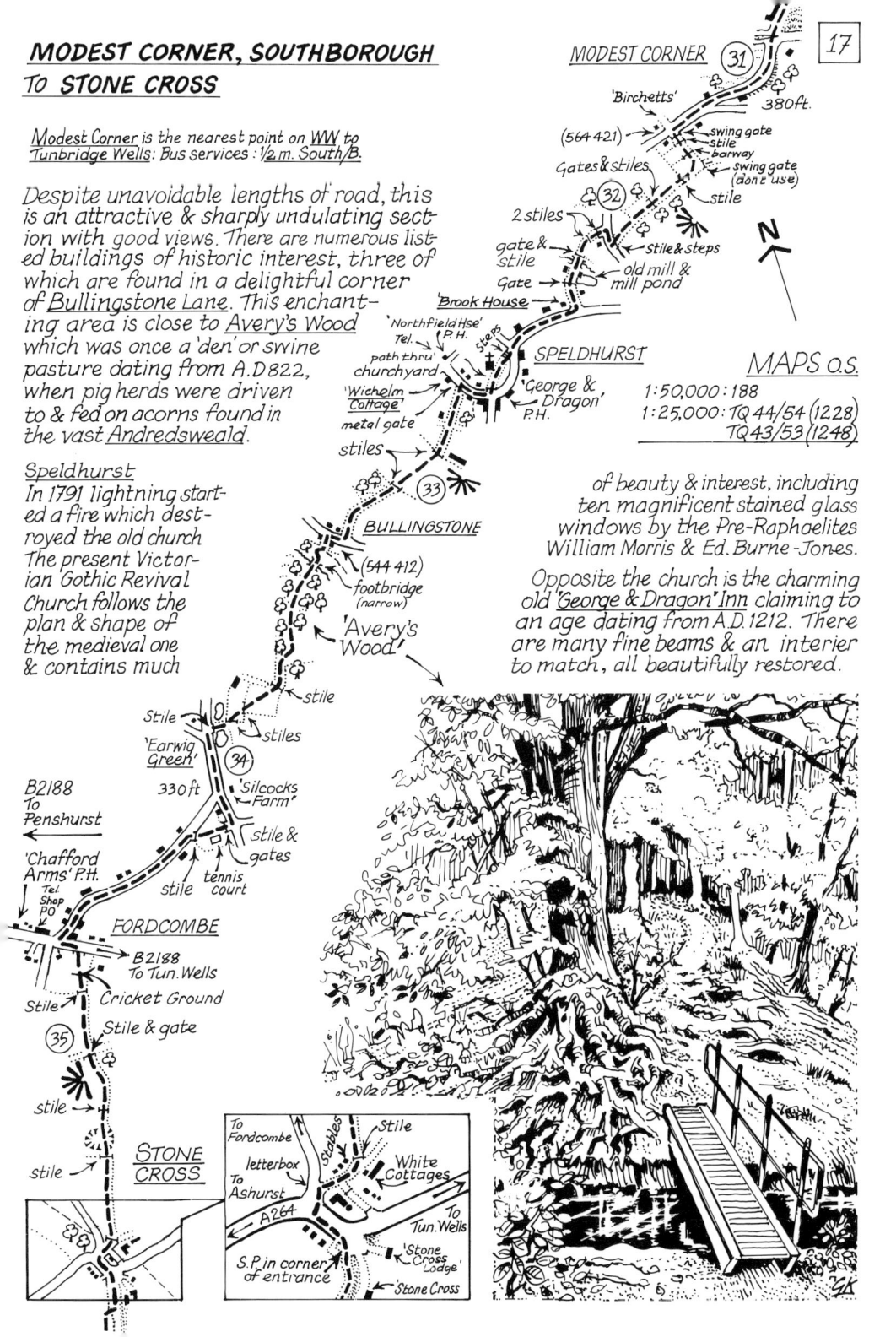

MODEST CORNER, SOUTHBOROUGH TO STONE CROSS

Modest Corner is the nearest point on WW to Tunbridge Wells: Bus services: ½ m. South/B.

Despite unavoidable lengths of road, this is an attractive & sharply undulating section with good views. There are numerous listed buildings of historic interest, three of which are found in a delightful corner of Bullingstone Lane. This enchanting area is close to Avery's Wood which was once a 'den' or swine pasture dating from A.D 822, when pig herds were driven to & fed on acorns found in the vast Andredsweald.

Speldhurst
In 1791 lightning started a fire which destroyed the old church. The present Victorian 'Gothic Revival' Church follows the plan & shape of the medieval one & contains much of beauty & interest, including ten magnificent stained glass windows by the Pre-Raphaelites William Morris & Ed. Burne-Jones.

Opposite the church is the charming old 'George & Dragon' Inn claiming to an age dating from A.D.1212. There are many fine beams & an interier to match, all beautifully restored.

MODEST CORNER (31) 380ft.
'Birchetts'
(564 421)
swing gate
stile
barway
swing gate (don't use)
Gates & stiles
stile
(32)
2 stiles
stile & steps
gate & stile
old mill & mill pond
Gate
'Brook House'
'Northfield Hse' Tel. P.H.
path thru churchyard
'Wichelm Cottage'
metal gate
SPELDHURST
'George & Dragon' P.H.
stiles

MAPS O.S.
1:50,000:188
1:25,000: TQ 44/54 (1228)
TQ 43/53 (1248)

(33)
BULLINGSTONE
(544 412)
footbridge (narrow)
'Avery's Wood'
stile
Stile
stiles
'Earwig Green'
(34)
330ft
'Silcocks Farm'
stile & gates
tennis court
stile

B2188 To Penshurst
'Chafford Arms' P.H.
Tel. Shop PO
FORDCOMBE
B2188 To Tun.Wells
Cricket Ground
Stile
Stile & gate
(35)
stile
stile

STONE CROSS
To Fordcombe
letterbox
To Ashurst
Stile
Stables
White Cottages
A264
To Tun. Wells
S.P. in corner of entrance
'Stone Cross Lodge'
'Stone Cross'

17

STONE CROSS TO WITHYHAM

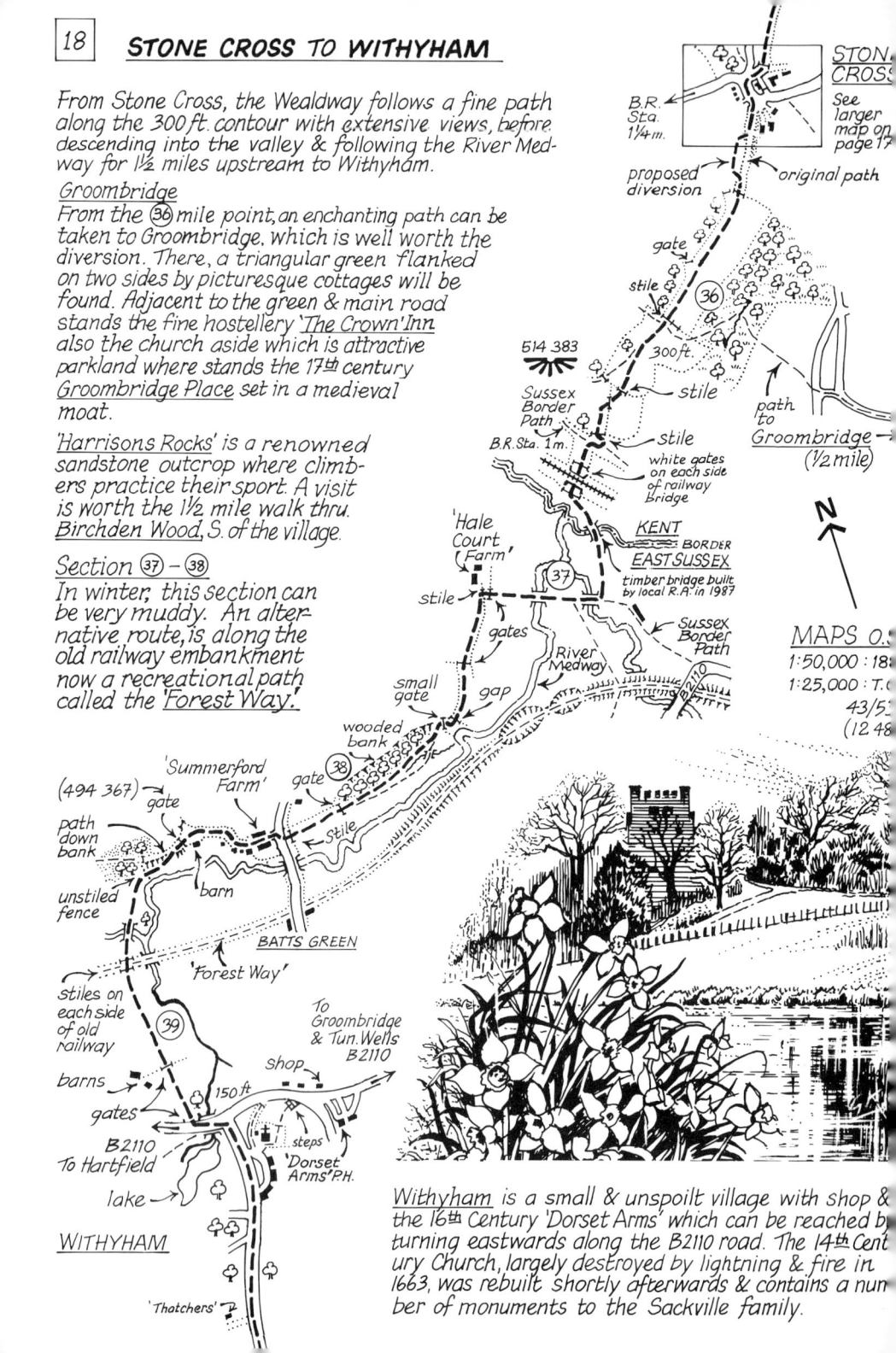

From Stone Cross, the Wealdway follows a fine path along the 300 ft. contour with extensive views, before descending into the valley & following the River Medway for 1½ miles upstream to Withyham.

Groombridge
From the (36) mile point, an enchanting path can be taken to Groombridge, which is well worth the diversion. There, a triangular green flanked on two sides by picturesque cottages will be found. Adjacent to the green & main road stands the fine hostellery 'The Crown' Inn also the church aside which is attractive parkland where stands the 17th century Groombridge Place set in a medieval moat.

'Harrisons Rocks' is a renowned sandstone outcrop where climbers practice their sport. A visit is worth the 1½ mile walk thru. Birchden Wood, S. of the village.

Section (37) – (38)
In winter, this section can be very muddy. An alternative route, is along the old railway embankment now a recreational path called the 'Forest Way.'

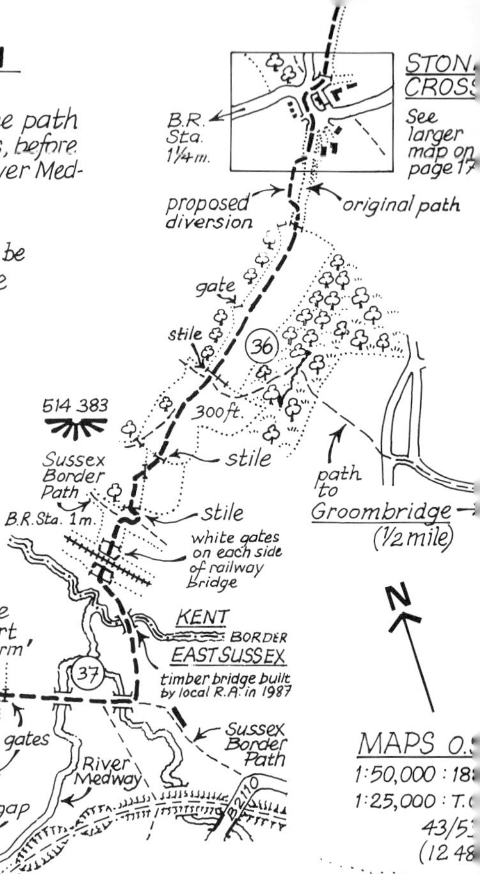
STONE CROSS
See larger map on page 17
B.R. Sta. 1¼ m.
proposed diversion
original path
gate
stile
36
514 383
300 ft.
stile
Sussex Border Path
B.R. Sta. 1 m.
stile
path to Groombridge (½ mile)
white gates on each side of railway bridge
KENT
BORDER
EAST SUSSEX
timber bridge built by local R.A. in 1987
'Hale Court Farm'
stile
37
gates
Sussex Border Path
River Medway
small gate
gap
B2110
MAPS O.S
1:50,000 : 18
1:25,000 : T.
43/5
(12 48

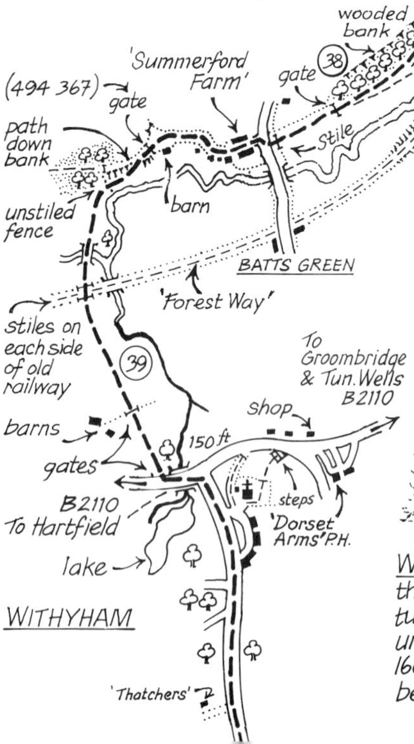
wooded bank
38
gate
'Summerford Farm'
(494 367)
gate
path down bank
Stile
barn
unstiled fence
BATTS GREEN
'Forest Way'
stiles on each side of old railway
39
To Groombridge & Tun. Wells B2110
shop
barns
150 ft
gates
B2110 To Hartfield
steps
'Dorset Arms' P.H.
lake
WITHYHAM
'Thatchers'

Withyham is a small & unspoilt village with shop & the 16th Century 'Dorset Arms' which can be reached by turning eastwards along the B2110 road. The 14th Century Church, largely destroyed by lightning & fire in 1663, was rebuilt shortly afterwards & contains a number of monuments to the Sackville family.

WEALDWAY ROUTE PLANNER

Approx. miles
N to S · S to N
(Accumulative)

Page	Map Ref.	Place Name · Miles between		N→S		S→N	
9	643 712 O.S.177	**GRAVESEND** (A2 Tollgate) To		4	4	78	◄ GRAVESEND TOWN MAP Page 8
10	670 663 O.S.177/188	**LUDDESDOWN** To		4	8	74	Notes _____
11	653 613 O.S.188	**TROTTISCLIFFE** (N.D.W) To		4	12	70	
12	626 568 O.S.188	**PLATT** To		5	17	66	
13	644 526 O.S.188	**WEST PECKHAM** To		4	21	61	
14 15	646 482 O.S.188	**BARNES STREET** To		5	26	57	◄ TONBRIDGE TOWN MAP Page 14
16	592 465 O.S.188	**TONBRIDGE** To		5	31	52	
17	572 423 O.S.188	**MODEST CORNER** To		5	36	47	
18	522 389 O.S.188	**STONE CROSS** To		4	40	42	
19	493 356 O.S.188	**WITHYHAM** To		3	43	38	
20	475 313 O.S.188	**TOP OF ASHDOWN FOREST** To (This name not on O.S. map)		3	46	35	
21	472 278 O.S.188/198	**BROWNS BROOK COTTAGE** To (This name not on O.S. map)		4	50	32	
22	487 234 O.S.198/199	**BUXTED PARK** To		4	54	28	◄ UCKFIELD TOWN MAP Page 23
24	516 205 O.S.199	**BLACKBOYS** To		4	58	24	
25	523 163 O.S.199	**EAST HOATHLY** To		3	61	20	
26	564 143 O.S.199	**GUN HILL** To		4	65	17	
27	576 104 O.S.199	**A22 (HAILSHAM)** To		3	68	13	
28	543 074 O.S.199	**ARLINGTON** To		5	73	10	
30	559 038 O.S.199	**FOLKINGTON** To EASTBOURNE		5	78	5	◄ EASTBOURNE TOWN MAP Page 31

Map Ref Nos are nearest points on route to Place Names
It is 2 miles to town centres at each end of Wealdway

PLACES OF INTEREST NEAR WEALDWAY

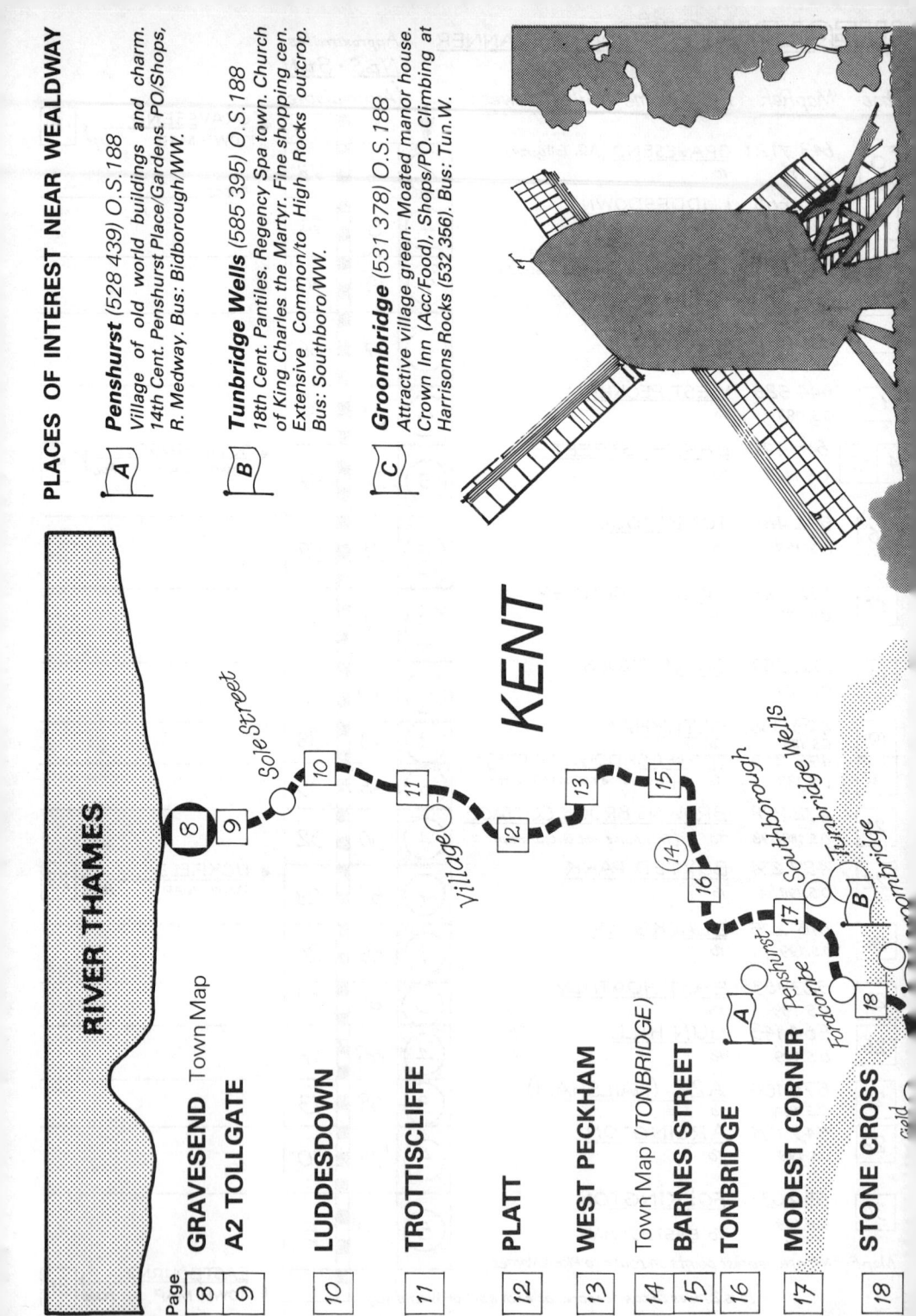

A **Penshurst** (528 439) O.S.188
Village of old world buildings and charm. 14th Cent. Penshurst Place/Gardens. PO/Shops, R. Medway. Bus: Bidborough/WW.

B **Tunbridge Wells** (585 395) O.S.188
18th Cent. Pantiles. Regency Spa town. Church of King Charles the Martyr. Fine shopping cen. Extensive Common/to High Rocks outcrop. Bus: Southboro/WW.

C **Groombridge** (531 378) O.S.188
Attractive village green. Moated manor house. Crown Inn (Acc/Food), Shops/PO. Climbing at Harrisons Rocks (532 356). Bus: Tun.W.

Page
- 8 — GRAVESEND Town Map
- 9 — A2 TOLLGATE
- 10 — LUDDESDOWN
- 11 — TROTTISCLIFFE
- 12 — PLATT
- 13 — WEST PECKHAM
- 14/15 — Town Map (TONBRIDGE)
- 16 — BARNES STREET / TONBRIDGE
- 17 — MODEST CORNER
- 18 — STONE CROSS

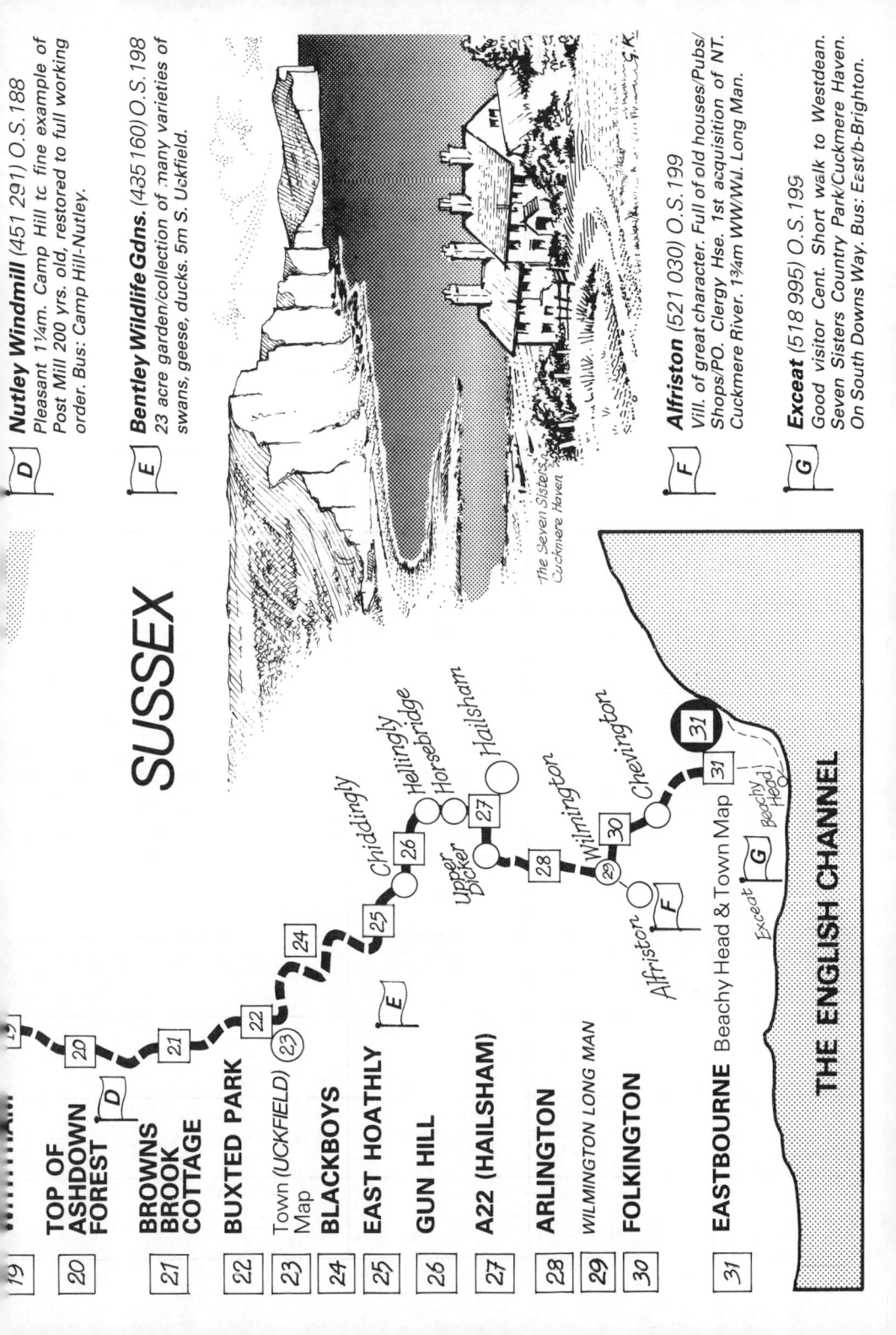

SUSSEX

D **Nutley Windmill** (451 291) O.S.188
Pleasant 1¼m. Camp Hill tc fine example of Post Mill 200 yrs. old, restored to full working order. Bus: Camp Hill-Nutley.

E **Bentley Wildlife Gdns.** (435 160) O.S.198
23 acre garden/collection of many varieties of swans, geese, ducks. 5m S. Uckfield.

F **Alfriston** (521 030) O.S.199
Vill. of great character. Full of old houses/Pubs/Shops/PO. Clergy Hse. 1st acquisition of NT. Cuckmere River. 1¾m WW/WJ. Long Man.

G **Exceat** (518 995) O.S.199
Good visitor Cent. Short walk to Westdean. Seven Sisters Country Park/Cuckmere Haven. On South Downs Way. Bus: East-b-Brighton.

19
20 TOP OF ASHDOWN FOREST
21 BROWNS BROOK COTTAGE
22 BUXTED PARK
23 Town (UCKFIELD) Map
24 BLACKBOYS
25 EAST HOATHLY
26 GUN HILL
27 A22 (HAILSHAM)
28 ARLINGTON
29 WILMINGTON LONG MAN
30 FOLKINGTON
31 EASTBOURNE Beachy Head & Town Map

THE ENGLISH CHANNEL

WEALDWAY ROUTE PLANNER · DIARY

Date	Miles	Start Place	Finish Place	Notes:

WITHYHAM TO TOP OF ASHDOWN FOREST | 19 |

From Withyham to Fisher's Gate, the Wealdway follows a metalled driveway. There are good views south to Ashdown Forest & north across the Medway Valley.

<u>Five Hundred Acre Wood</u> was first enclosed in 1693 and the fine oak and beech are a legacy from early plantings. The wood has since become well known as the setting for AA Milne's Christopher Robin books. The path through the wood was dedicated as a right of way by the landowner as a contribution to European Conservation Year 1970. Unfortunately many trees were lost in the October 1987 devastating hurricane. At Greenwood Gate Clump, the Wealdway reaches its highest point at 720ft, as it crosses the top of the sandstone forest ridge.

<u>MAPS</u> O.S. 1:50,000 : 188
1:25,000 : TQ43/53
(12.48)

'Five Hundred Acre Wood'

Standing 30" high these natural oak posts are placed discreetly.

ROUTE FINDING

<u>A→B</u> <u>B→A</u>: It is easy to get lost in 500 Acre Wood. There is a sign at 'A' indicating the start of the path up through the wood.

<u>B→C</u> <u>C→B</u>: Crosses open forest & there are no clear landmarks. The B2188 is never far away and the heading is app. North-South. Look out for the special Wealdway waymark posts on Ashdown Forest. The route in each direction is indicated on top of the post. (See sketch at left).

20

TOP OF ASHDOWN FOREST TO BROWNS BROOK COTTAGE

In Roman times the huge Wealden forest of Anderida, stretched for more than 100 miles over south east England. Ashdown Forest is the largest remaining part but today its appearance must be very different; now a wild area of heath, moorland, rocky outcrops and woodland. The furnaces of the great Sussex iron industry were fed by the timber felled in the forest and the many hammer ponds dammed to drive the forge hammers, are now all that remains to remind us of this important era in Wealden history.

The medieval forest of Ashdown occupied over 15,000 acres and was created as a Royal hunting ground, but officially dis-afforested in 1662.

The high ground between Five Hundred Acre Wood and Camp Hill is superb open heathland, under the control of the Conservators of Ashdown Forest but is open for public access.

Camp Hill, in fair weather, is a good spot for a break and picnic, from here there are extensive views south across the Clay Weald to the South Downs. Descending to Oldlands Corner, the route has to circumvent a number of small cottages built on land carved piece-meal from the forest as a result of 17th Century clearance and enclosure.

MAPS 1:50,000 : 188
O.S. 1:25,000 : TQ43/53 (12.48)
TQ42/52 (12.69)

ROUTE FINDING
A→B→C C→B→A In clear weather, Camp Hill is a good landmark for southbound walkers (aim for clump of conifers. See map at C).

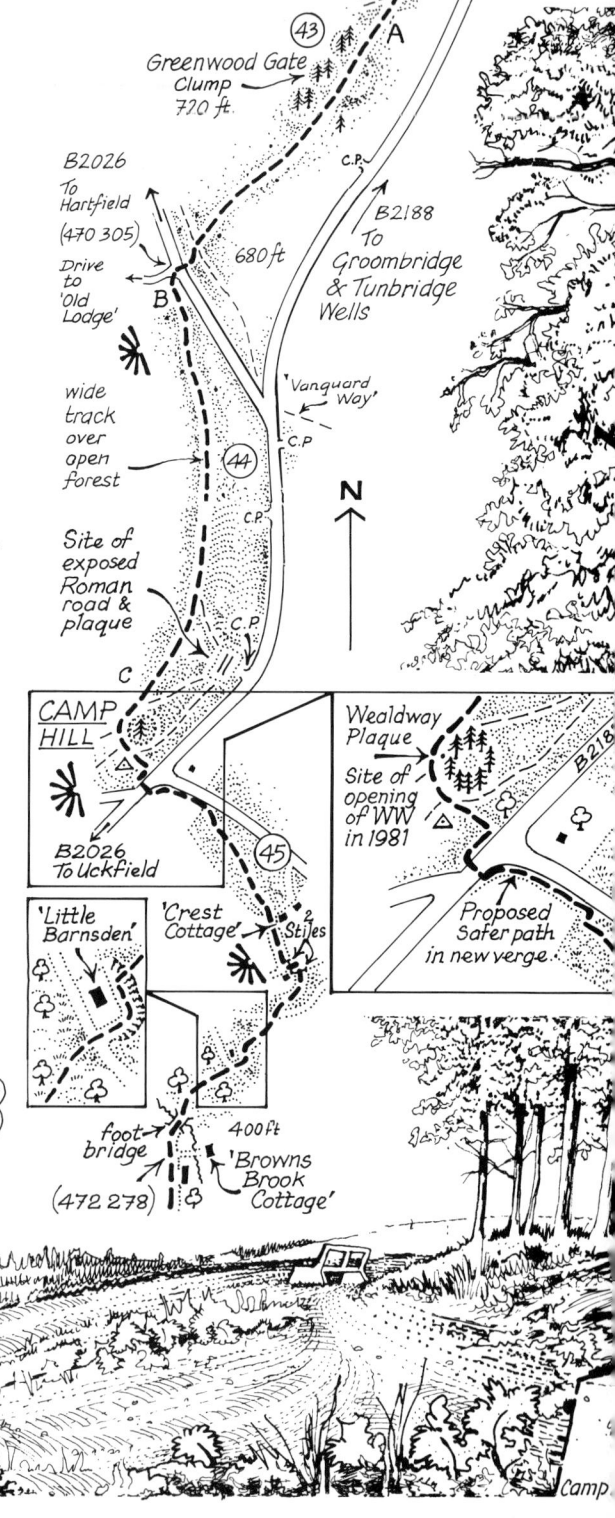

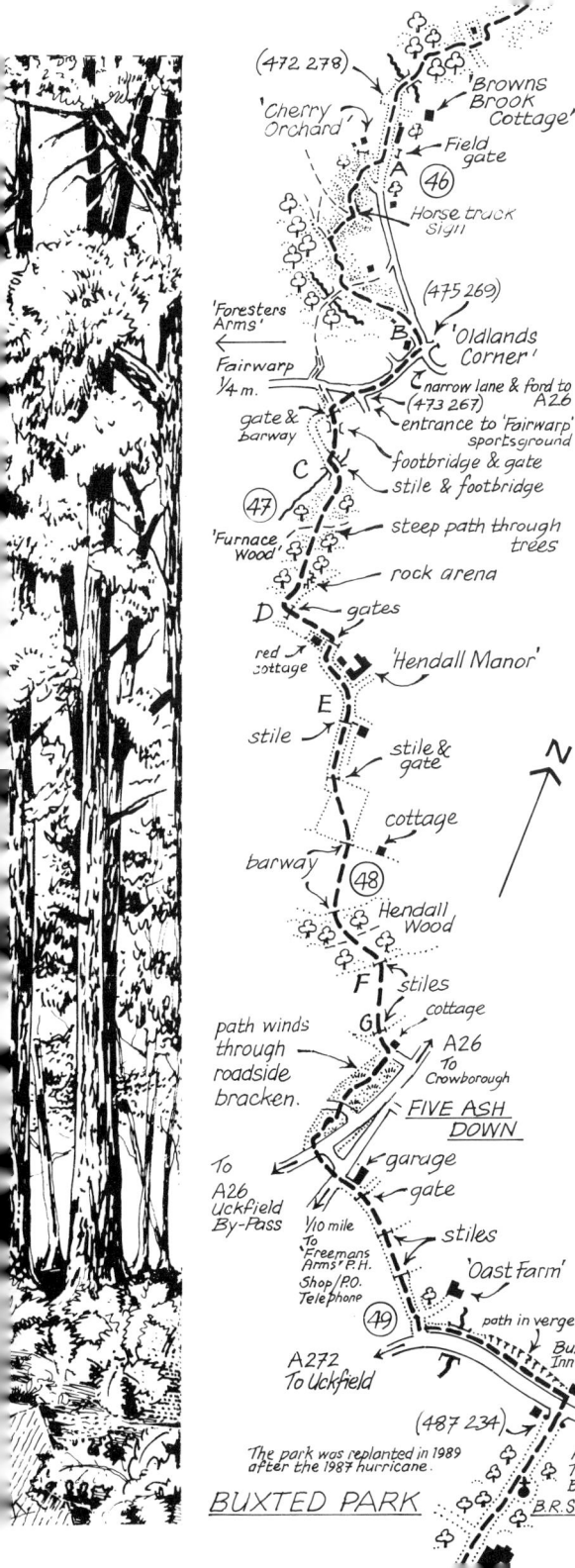

BROWNS BROOK COTTAGE TO BUXTED PARK

<u>Furnace Wood</u>, an area of mixed woodland under the management of the Forestry Commission, provides welcome shade after the open acres of the Forest. The name provides a reminder that this is Wealden Iron Country. The 1987 hurricane took its toll of many trees in this area.

<u>Hendall Wood</u>, further south, has been extensively clear felled in recent years, though a reasonably generous strip has been preserved, at least for the time being.

<u>MAPS</u>   O.S. 1:50,000 : 188, 198
              1:25,000 : TQ 42/52
<u>ROUTE FINDING</u> (12.69)

<u>A→B</u>: At 'A' turn uphill on narrow path. Cross access drive to 'Cherry Orchard' & bear slightly left onto narrow path through gorse. When reaching a broad ride, turn left onto it & in about 150 paces, turn right on narrow path towards trees. At trees, turn left on path & in about 300 paces reach a bridge. (Seen on rt. do not cross). Continue, bearing slightly left ahead to Oldlands Corner.

<u>B→A</u>: 100 yds from Oldlands Corner fork left by garages & take path through gorse to footbridge (Seen on left do not cross). Continue winding path (trees to left) & in 300 paces turn rt. uphill on narrow path thro' gorse. At broad ride, turn left onto it for 150 paces & then rt. on narrow path to 'Cherry Orchard' access drive. Cross to narrow downhill path to track.

<u>C→D D→C</u>: There are alternatives through Furnace Wood but the correct path is waymarked.

<u>D→E</u>: Keep left of red cottage & turn right beyond it to join drive, keeping right of Hendall Farm House.

<u>E→D</u>: On drive, pass left of Hendall Farm House to red cottage, go thru' gate at right & pass behind cottage.

<u>F→G G→F</u>: Take a near North/South line across field.

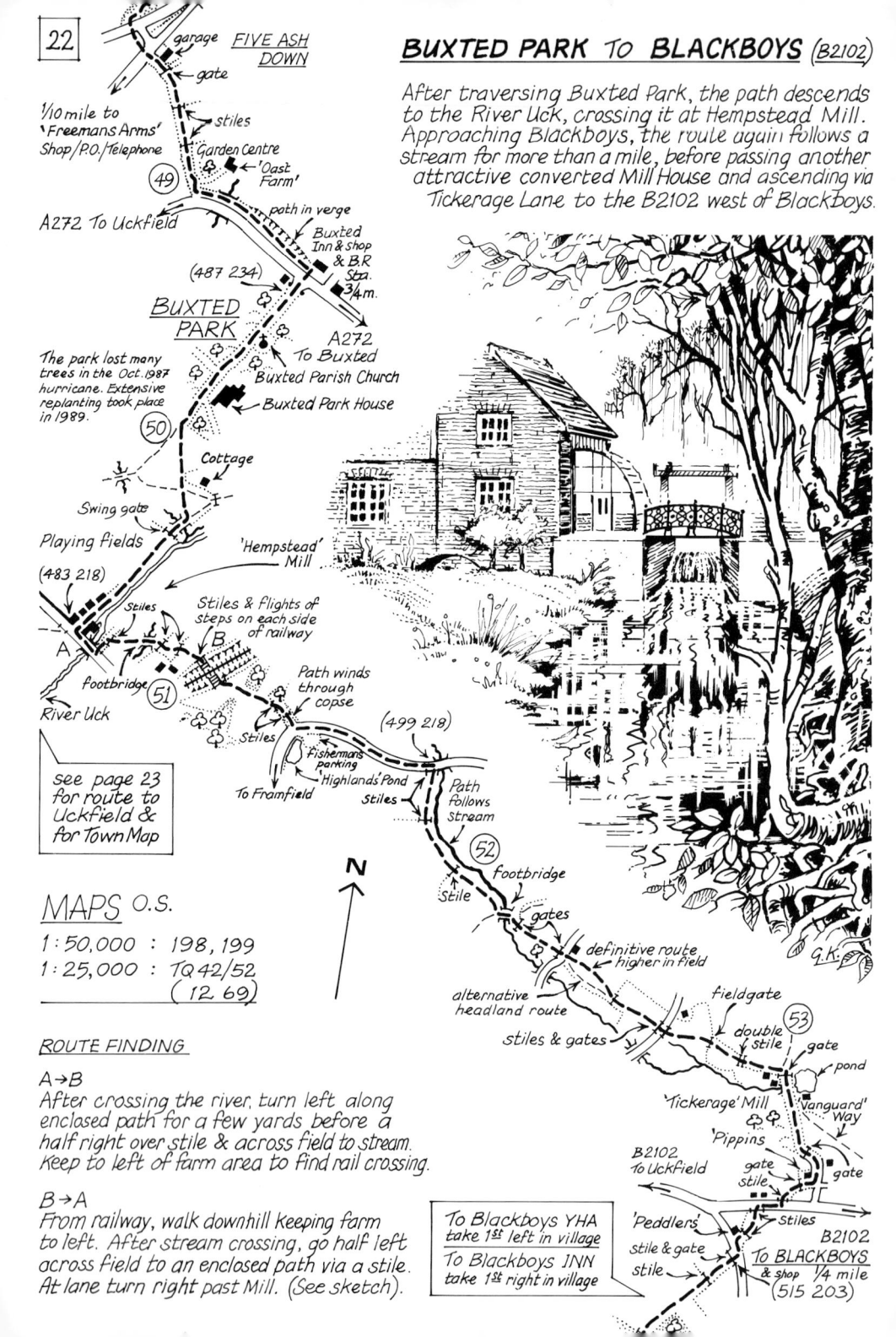

BUXTED PARK TO BLACKBOYS (B2102)

After traversing Buxted Park, the path descends to the River Uck, crossing it at Hempstead Mill. Approaching Blackboys, the route again follows a stream for more than a mile, before passing another attractive converted Mill House and ascending via Tickerage Lane to the B2102 west of Blackboys.

FIVE ASH DOWN
- garage
- gate
- 1/10 mile to 'Freemans Arms' Shop/P.O./Telephone
- stiles
- Garden Centre
- 'Oast Farm'
- (49)
- A272 To Uckfield
- path in verge
- Buxted Inn & shop & B.R. Sta. 3/4 m.
- (487 234)
- A272 To Buxted

BUXTED PARK

The park lost many trees in the Oct. 1987 hurricane. Extensive replanting took place in 1989.

- Buxted Parish Church
- Buxted Park House
- (50)
- Cottage
- Swing gate
- Playing fields (483 218)
- Stiles
- A
- footbridge (51)
- River Uck
- B
- Stiles & flights of steps on each side of railway
- 'Hempstead' Mill
- Path winds through copse
- Stiles
- Fishermans parking
- To Framfield
- Highlands Pond
- (499 218)
- Stiles
- Path follows Stream
- (52) footbridge
- Stile
- gates
- definitive route higher in field
- alternative headland route
- stiles & gates
- fieldgate
- double stile
- (53)
- gate
- pond
- 'Tickerage' Mill
- 'Vanguard' Way
- 'Pippins'
- B2102 To Uckfield
- gate stile
- gate
- 'Peddlers'
- stile & gate
- stile
- stiles
- B2102 To BLACKBOYS & shop 1/4 mile (515 203)

see page 23 for route to Uckfield & for Town Map

N →

MAPS O.S.
1:50,000 : 198, 199
1:25,000 : TQ 42/52 (12.69)

ROUTE FINDING

A → B
After crossing the river, turn left along enclosed path for a few yards before a half right over stile & across field to stream. Keep to left of farm area to find rail crossing.

B → A
From railway, walk downhill keeping farm to left. After stream crossing, go half left across field to an enclosed path via a stile. At lane turn right past Mill. (See sketch).

To Blackboys YHA take 1st left in village
To Blackboys INN take 1st right in village

G.K.

22

UCKFIELD TOWN MAP with route from Wealdway to the town High Street [23]

Uckfield, a much expanded town in recent years, is the second of the two intermediary towns on Wealdway, the main route of which turns abruptly east at Hempstead Mill. Turning west, the walker seeking refreshment & public transport, can soon reach the town High St., via Hempstead Lane.

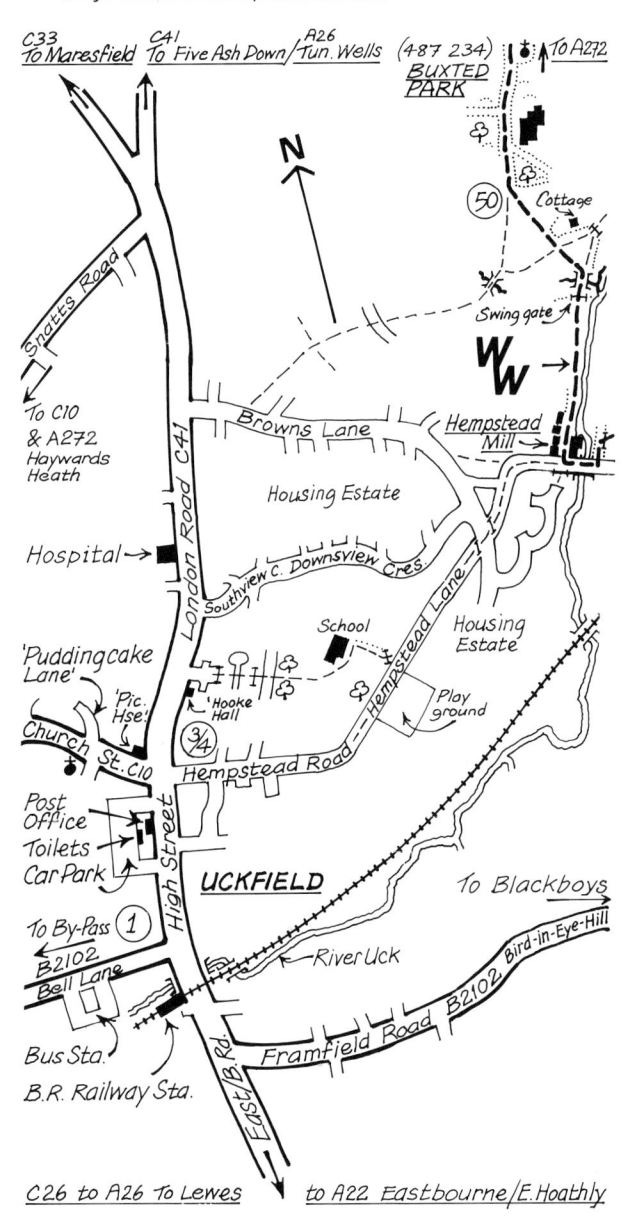

'Hooke Hall' · High Street · Uckfield

There are various interesting brick, weatherboarded & tilehung buildings including the bow windowed Georgian 'Maidens Head' pub with quiet corners like 'Monks Walk' and Puddingcake Lane, all found in the older northern part of town. The restored 'Bridge Cottage', a fine old timber framed Wealden Hall, open to the public, can be found at the bottom of the High Street near to the bus & British Rail stations. Almost unique in country towns of today, is the recently refurbished High Street 'Picture House,' still a popular cinema showing the latest attractions of the silver screen.

Scale: 1/4 mile   MAPS O.S. 50,000 : 198
                              25,000 : TQ42/52 (12 69)

24 BLACKBOYS TO EAST HOATHLY

After passing the landscaped gardens of New Place, the path crosses open farmland before traversing the sad remains of Great Wood, clear felled in recent years. The 1987 hurricane felled much of the remaining woodland.

East Hoathly
In 1856 the church was largely rebuilt but the 15th Century tower was retained. The Tudor doorway is ornamented by the Pelham Buckle, a sword buckle presented to the family by John of France, after the battle of Poitiers. The remains of the Pelham family seat are incorporated into nearby Halland Park Farm. A planned by-pass will soon restore quiet to the village.

MAPS O.S.
1:50,000:199
1:25,000:T.Q.
42/52 (1269)
41/51 (1289)

ROUTE FINDING
A→B & B→A There are no obvious landmarks across this clear-felled area.
A→B From stream, head uphill into field, at appro. centre, turn right to hedge where a double stile is crossed. Then head to the left of the middle of 3 pylons.
B→A From wood aim to right of the middle of 3 pylons. Then head for double stile in hedgerow, enter field to approx. centre, the route then turns left to A (Hidden stream).

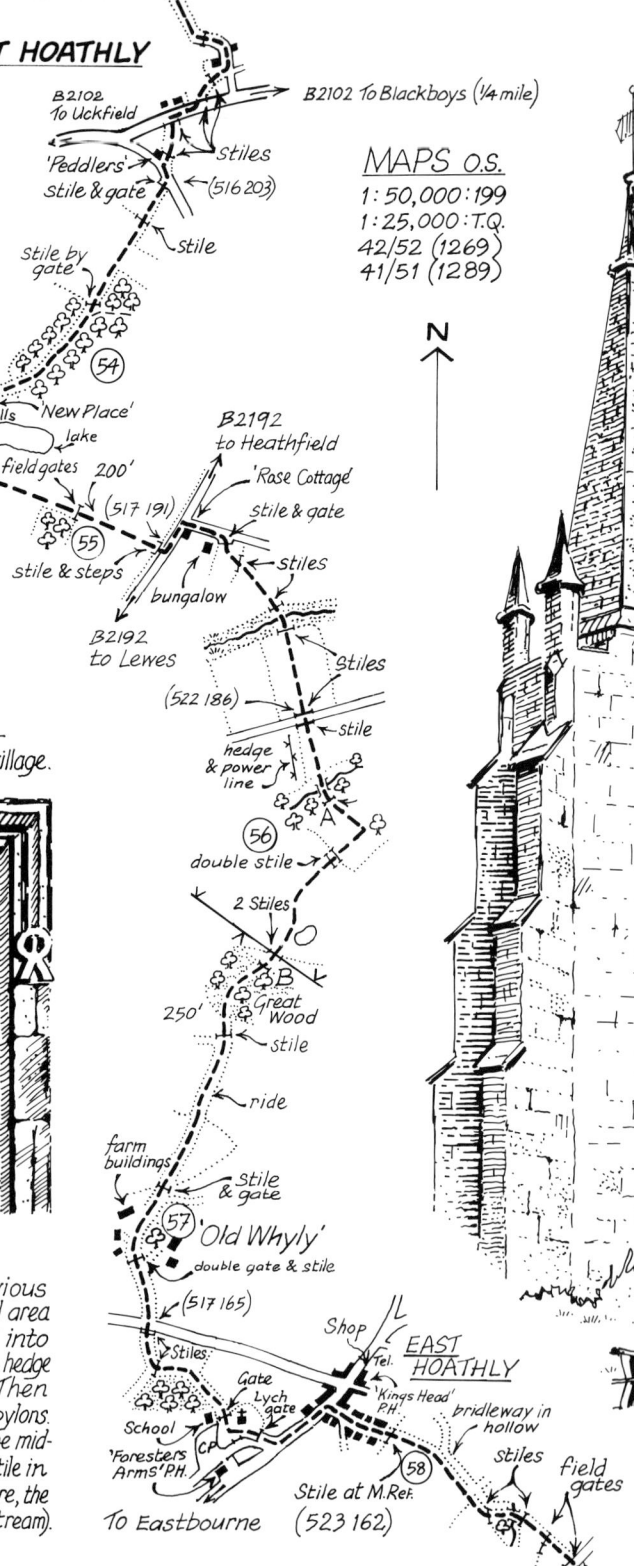

EAST HOATHLY TO GUN HILL [25]

EAST HOATHLY

A very pleasant field path route across undulating, typically Wealden countryside, a contrasting mixture of arable and pasture interspersed with small coppices and streams. There are good views south to the Downs from a number of vantage points on clear days, including <u>Chiddingly</u> churchyard.

The Tudor remains of <u>Chiddingly Place</u>, home of Jeffery family, have been incorporated into a farmhouse which adjoins the Wealdway route. The church contains a large monument to Sir John Jeffery, a baron of the exchequer in the reign of Elizabeth I.

Gatehouse Farm

MAPS O.S.
1:50,000 : 199
1:25,000 : T.Q.
41/51 (1289)

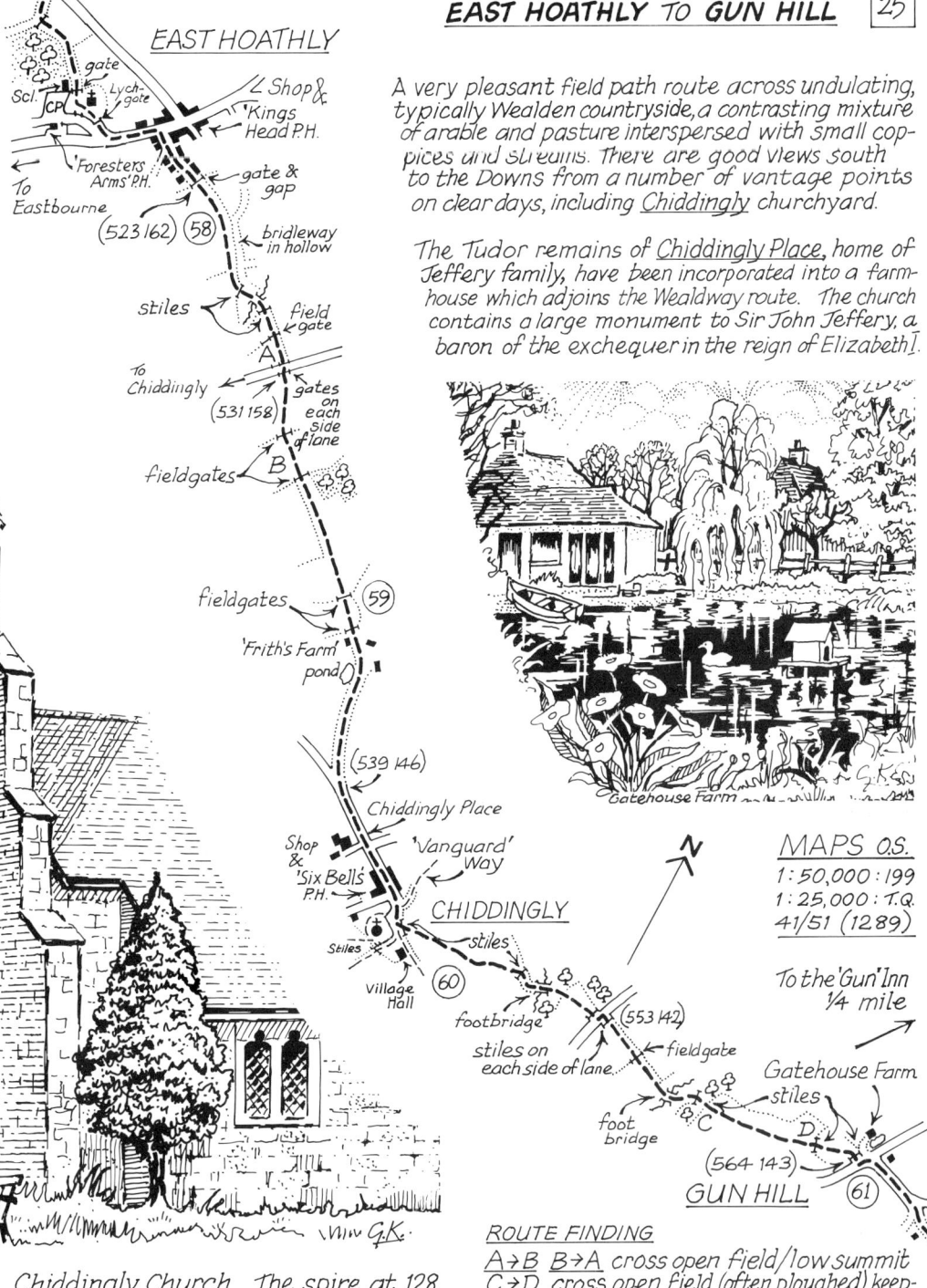

To the 'Gun' Inn ¼ mile

GUN HILL

Chiddingly Church. The spire at 128 feet is one of five similar Sussex spires. It dominates the area and provides a conspicuous landmark for all walkers.

ROUTE FINDING
A→B B→A cross open field / low summit
C→D cross open field (often ploughed) keeping parallel to woodland on your left.
D→C cross open field (often ploughed) aiming for the spire of <u>Chiddingly Church</u>.

26

GUN HILL TO A22 (Nr. HAILSHAM)

MAPS O.S.
1:50,000 : 199
1:25,000 : TQ
41/51 (12 89)

After crossing pleasant rolling farmland S.E. from Gun Hill, the route descends into the Cuckmere Valley at Hellingly, keeping alongside the river to Horsebridge.

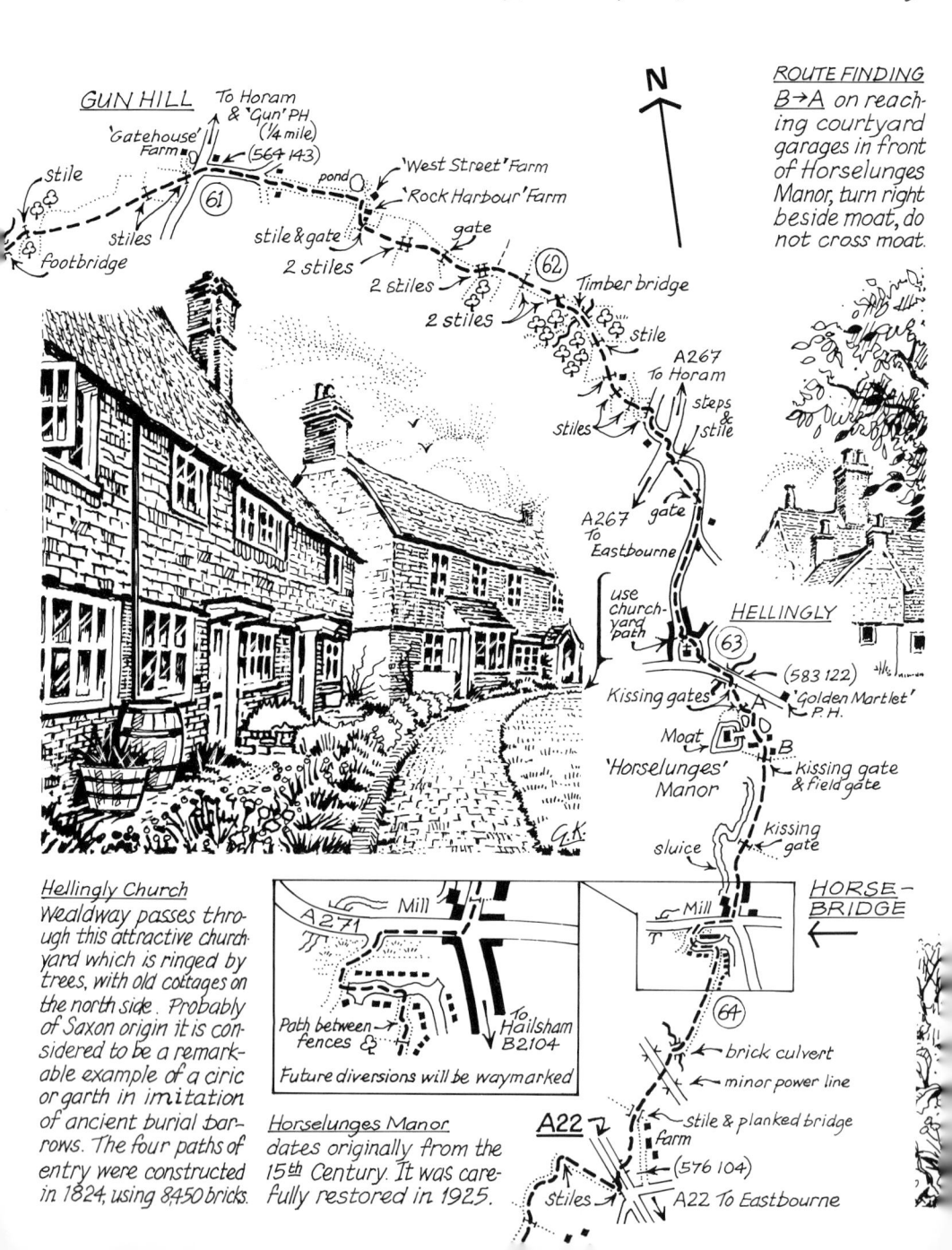

ROUTE FINDING
B→A on reaching courtyard garages in front of Horselunges Manor, turn right beside moat, do not cross moat.

GUN HILL
To Horam & 'Gun' P.H. (¼ mile) (564 143)
'Gatehouse' Farm
stile
stiles
footbridge
(61)
pond
stile & gate
2 stiles
'West Street' Farm
'Rock Harbour' Farm
gate
2 stiles
2 stiles
(62)
Timber bridge
stile
A267 To Horam
steps & stile
stiles
A267 To Eastbourne
gate
use churchyard path
HELLINGLY
(63)
(583 122)
'Golden Martlet' P.H.
Kissing gates
A
Moat
'Horselunges' Manor
B
kissing gate & field gate
sluice
kissing gate
Mill
Mill
HORSE-BRIDGE
A271
Path between fences
To Hailsham B2104
Future diversions will be waymarked
(64)
brick culvert
minor power line
stile & planked bridge
farm
(576 104)
A22
stiles
A22 To Eastbourne

Hellingly Church
Wealdway passes through this attractive churchyard which is ringed by trees, with old cottages on the north side. Probably of Saxon origin it is considered to be a remarkable example of a ciric or garth in imitation of ancient burial barrows. The four paths of entry were constructed in 1824, using 8,450 bricks.

Horselunges Manor dates originally from the 15th Century. It was carefully restored in 1925.

A22 (NR. HAILSHAM) to ARLINGTON

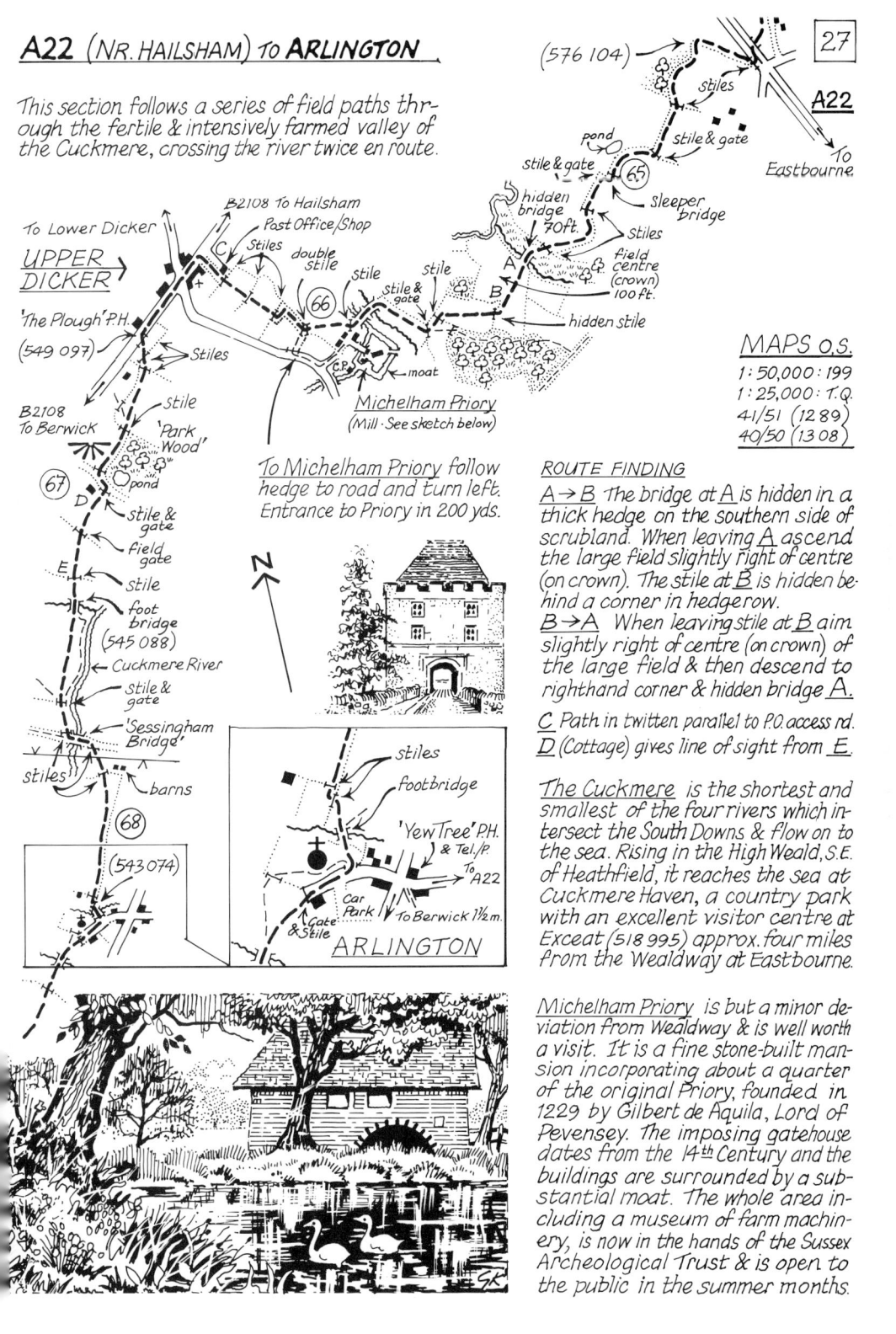

This section follows a series of field paths through the fertile & intensively farmed valley of the Cuckmere, crossing the river twice en route.

27

(576 104)

A22 To Eastbourne

To Lower Dicker
UPPER DICKER
B2108 To Hailsham
Post Office/Shop
stiles
double stile
stile
stile
stile & gate
'The Plough' P.H. (549 097)
Stiles
B2108 To Berwick
stile
'Park Wood'
pond
(67)
D
stile & gate
field gate
E
stile
foot bridge (545 088)
Cuckmere River
Stile & gate
'Sessingham Bridge'
stiles
barns
(68)
(543 074)

(66)
C.P.
moat
Michelham Priory
(Mill · See sketch below)

pond
stile & gate
hidden bridge 70ft
stiles
A
B
(65)
stile & gate
stiles
sleeper bridge
field centre (crown) 100 ft
hidden stile

stiles
footbridge
'Yew Tree' P.H. & Tel./P.
To A22
Car Park
Gate & Stile
To Berwick 1½ m.
ARLINGTON

To Michelham Priory follow hedge to road and turn left. Entrance to Priory in 200 yds.

MAPS O.S.
1:50,000:199
1:25,000: T.Q.
41/51 (1289)
40/50 (1308)

ROUTE FINDING

A→B The bridge at A is hidden in a thick hedge on the southern side of scrubland. When leaving A, ascend the large field slightly right of centre (on crown). The stile at B is hidden behind a corner in hedgerow.

B→A When leaving stile at B aim slightly right of centre (on crown) of the large field & then descend to righthand corner & hidden bridge A.

C Path in twitten parallel to P.O. access rd.
D (Cottage) gives line of sight from E.

The Cuckmere is the shortest and smallest of the four rivers which intersect the South Downs & flow on to the sea. Rising in the High Weald, S.E. of Heathfield, it reaches the sea at Cuckmere Haven, a country park with an excellent visitor centre at Exceat (518 995) approx. four miles from the Wealdway at Eastbourne.

Michelham Priory is but a minor deviation from Wealdway & is well worth a visit. It is a fine stone-built mansion incorporating about a quarter of the original Priory, founded in 1229 by Gilbert de Aquila, Lord of Pevensey. The imposing gatehouse dates from the 14th Century and the buildings are surrounded by a substantial moat. The whole area including a museum of farm machinery, is now in the hands of the Sussex Archeological Trust & is open to the public in the summer months.

28 ARLINGTON TO FOLKINGTON

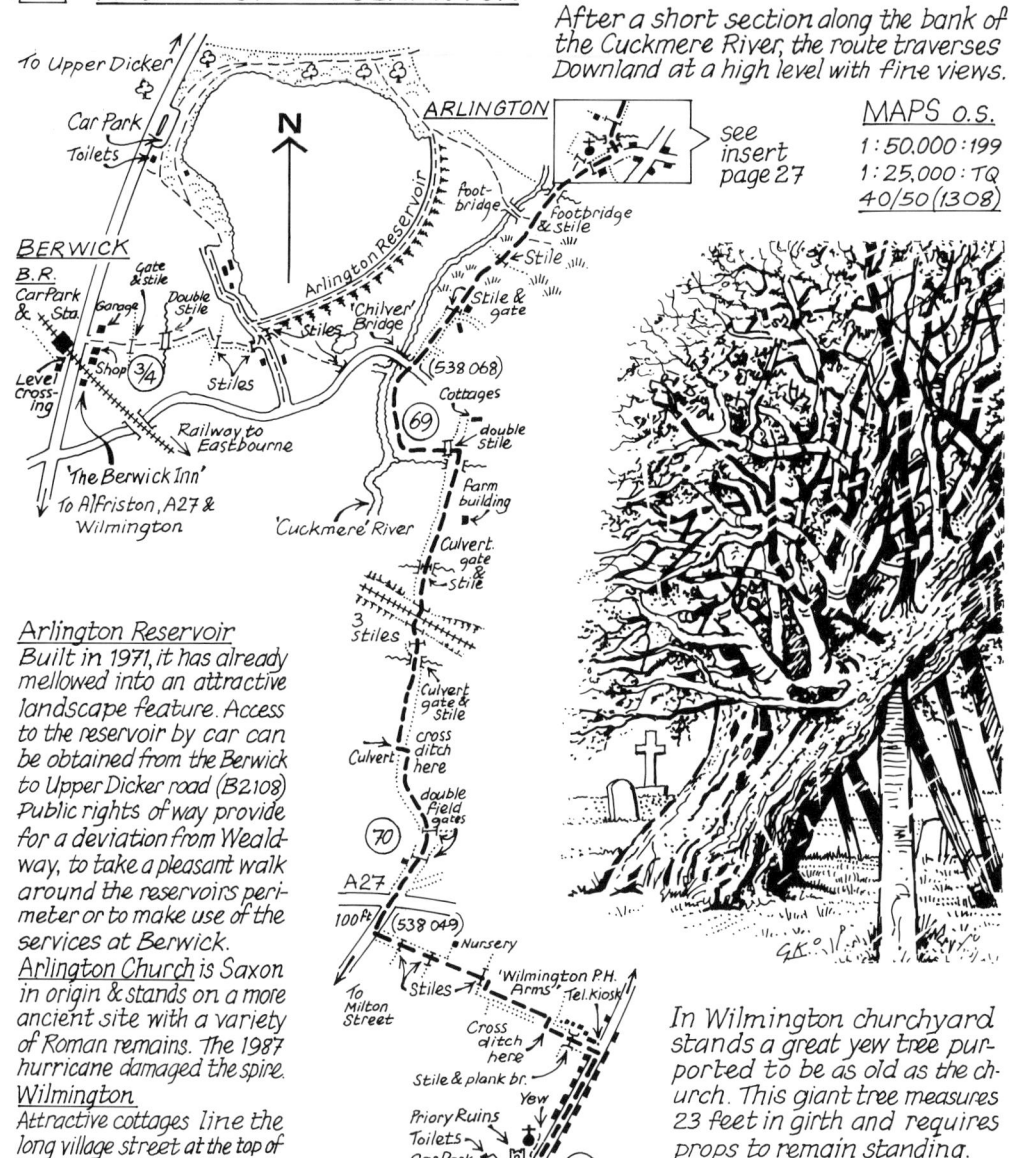

After a short section along the bank of the Cuckmere River, the route traverses Downland at a high level with fine views.

see insert page 27

MAPS O.S.
1:50,000 : 199
1:25,000 : TQ
40/50 (1308)

Arlington Reservoir
Built in 1971, it has already mellowed into an attractive landscape feature. Access to the reservoir by car can be obtained from the Berwick to Upper Dicker road (B2108). Public rights of way provide for a deviation from Wealdway, to take a pleasant walk around the reservoirs perimeter or to make use of the services at Berwick.

Arlington Church is Saxon in origin & stands on a more ancient site with a variety of Roman remains. The 1987 hurricane damaged the spire.

Wilmington
Attractive cottages line the long village street at the top of which stands the ruin of the 13th Century Priory now in the care of the Sussex Archeological Society. They open to the public at certain times. Close by is a convenient car park & plaque to view the distant Long Man of Wilmington. At 226 ft. high it is the largest known artifact of it's kind, in the Western hemisphere.

In Wilmington churchyard stands a great yew tree purported to be as old as the church. This giant tree measures 23 feet in girth and requires props to remain standing.

The Long Man can be viewed from above by deviating from Wealdway along the path system shown.

Long Man of Wilmington.

At Wilmington Priory, walkers obtain a magnificent view of the Long Man. As shown in the key map below, the route traverses near to the foot of the carving.

(See opposite page/map and 'Further Reading' page 35)

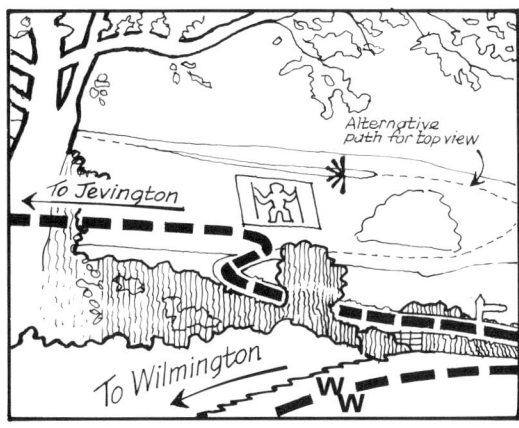

30 FOLKINGTON to EASTBOURNE (Y.H.A.)

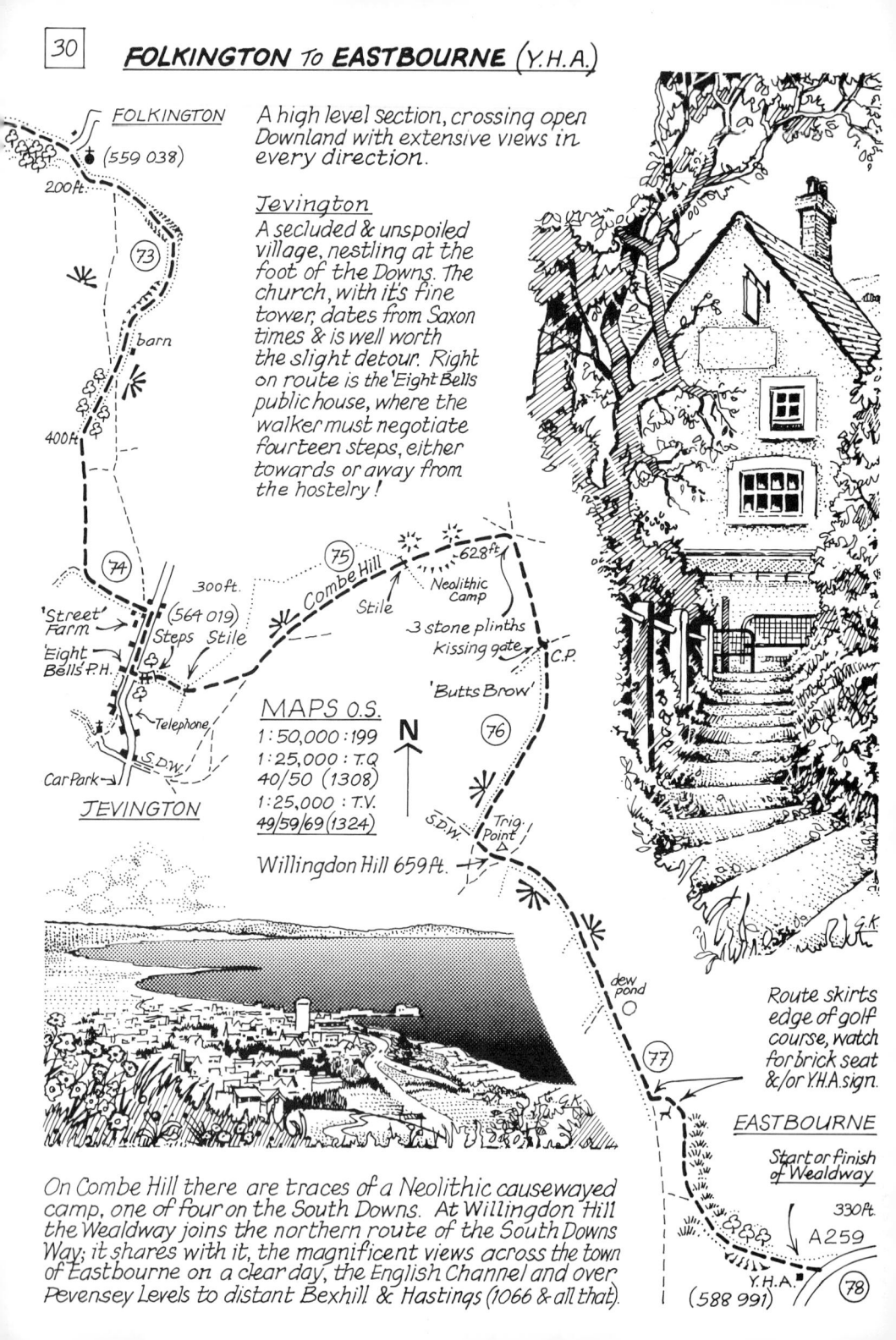

A high level section, crossing open Downland with extensive views in every direction.

Jevington

A secluded & unspoiled village, nestling at the foot of the Downs. The church, with it's fine tower, dates from Saxon times & is well worth the slight detour. Right on route is the 'Eight Bells' public house, where the walker must negotiate fourteen steps, either towards or away from the hostelry!

FOLKINGTON (559 038)

MAPS O.S.
1:50,000 : 199
1:25,000 : T.Q 40/50 (1308)
1:25,000 : T.V. 49/59/69 (1324)

Willingdon Hill 659 ft.

'Street' Farm — 'Eight Bells' P.H. — Telephone — Car Park — JEVINGTON

300 ft. (564 019) Steps Stile — Combe Hill — Stile — 628 ft. Neolithic Camp — 3 stone plinths kissing gate — C.P. — 'Butts Brow' — Trig Point — S.D.W. — dew pond

Route skirts edge of golf course, watch for brick seat &/or Y.H.A. sign.

EASTBOURNE
Start or finish of Wealdway

330 ft. A259
Y.H.A. (588 991)

On Combe Hill there are traces of a Neolithic causewayed camp, one of four on the South Downs. At Willingdon Hill the Wealdway joins the northern route of the South Downs Way; it shares with it, the magnificent views across the town of Eastbourne on a clear day, the English Channel and over Pevensey Levels to distant Bexhill & Hastings (1066 & all that).

EASTBOURNE TOWN MAP — 31

Eastbourne is an excellent start or finish for the Wealdway with good rail, bus and nearby ferry port services.

An attractive town still retaining the charm and elegance designed by the 7th Duke of Devonshire in the 19th Cent. E. also has long days of sun.

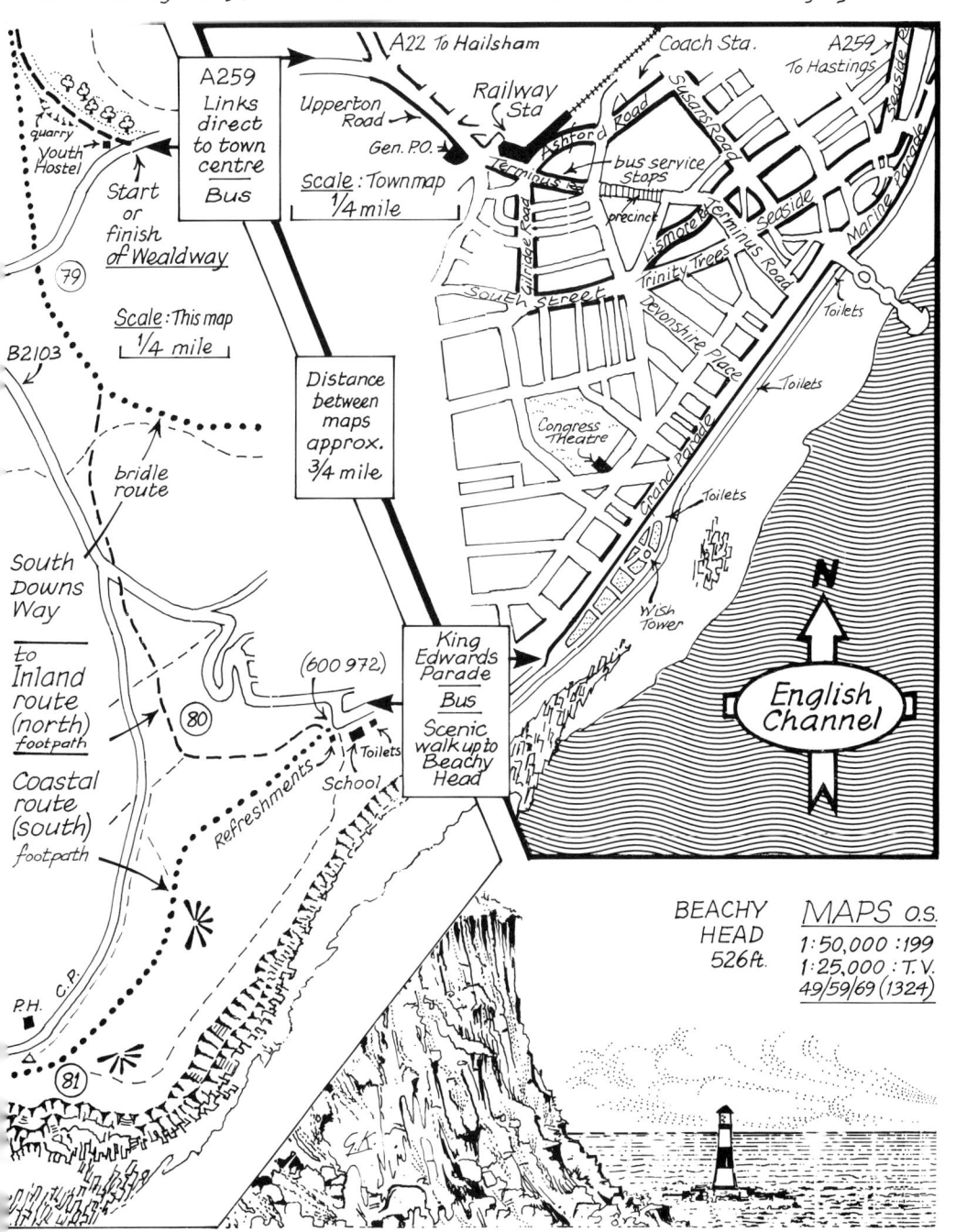

A259 Links direct to town centre — Bus

Start or finish of Wealdway

quarry, Youth Hostel

A22 To Hailsham
Upperton Road
Gen. P.O.
Railway Sta.
Coach Sta.
A259 To Hastings
Ashford Road
Susans Road
bus service Stops
Terminus Road
precinct
Lismore Road
Seaside
Marine Parade
Trinity Trees
South Street
Devonshire Place
Toilets
Congress Theatre
Grand Parade
Toilets
Wish Tower
Toilets

Scale: Townmap ¼ mile

Scale: This map ¼ mile

B2103

bridle route

Distance between maps approx. ¾ mile

South Downs Way
to Inland route (north) footpath
Coastal route (south) footpath

(79)
(80)
(600 972)
Refreshments
Toilets
School

King Edwards Parade — Bus — Scenic walk up to Beachy Head

N ↑ English Channel

P.H. C.P.
(81)

BEACHY HEAD 526 ft.

MAPS O.S.
1:50,000 : 199
1:25,000 : T.V. 49/59/69 (1324)

THE RAMBLERS' ASSOCIATION

Founded in 1935, the Ramblers' Association is a registered charity with four main aims. It promotes walking, protects rights of way, campaigns for access to open country and defends the beauty of the countryside. There are over 320 local RA groups throughout England, Scotland and Wales, which organise programmes of walks and other social activities, as well as carrying out vital footpath and countryside work.

At the beginning of 1990 there were 75,000 members, twice as many as a decade ago. The more people we speak for, the more our views will be listened to. So if you share our concerns, please add your weight to our numbers.

When you join, some very worthwhile benefits come your way, including: *The Rambler's Yearbook*, full of bed and breakfast addresses as well as useful information on long distance paths, maps etc.; regular campaign broadsheets; regional newsletters; use of our 1:50,000 Ordnance Survey map library; and special discounts at leading outdoor equipment shops.

THE BENEFITS OF MEMBERSHIP

1. The 'Ramblers' colour magazine
2. The Rambler's Yearbook
3. Membership of Local Groups
4. Regular Campaign Broadsheets
5. Use of Library
6. Regional Newsletters
7. Discounts
8. Your valuable support

RAMBLERS' ASSOCIATION · APPLICATION FOR MEMBERSHIP

To: The Ramblers' Association, 1/5 Wandsworth Road, London SW8 2XX

I/We wish to join the Ramblers' Association and have ticked the type of membership required.

DATE OF BIRTH	Mr/Mrs/Miss/Ms (INITIALS)
	SURNAME
RA GROUP (If you have a preference)	ADDRESS
	COUNTY POST CODE

Free junior membership cards can be issued for each child under 16 on receipt of a stamped addressed envelope.

Tick box suiting you best   £ . p

Individual Membership
- ☐ ORDINARY   £12.00 _____
- ☐ REDUCED*   £6.00 _____
- ☐ LIFE   £420.00 _____

Family or joint membership (for two members at the same address).
- ☐ ORDINARY   £15.00 _____
- ☐ REDUCED   £7.50 _____

☐ DONATION (To Countryside Fund) _____

☐ TOTAL ENCLOSED   : _____

* Reduced rates for members under 18, students, retired, disabled or unwaged. This rate does not apply to people outside the UK. Subscription rates effective until 1st October 1990.

Please ensure you sign your cheque and place it with this completed form into a stamped envelope addressed to the Ramblers' Association as above.

Please help us to save money

Your signing of a DIRECT DEBIT instruction can minimise our administrative costs, which saves time and money for you and us. The instruction is for a variable amount because the subscriptions usually increase annually, thus you are spared the inconvenience of completing a new instruction each year. You are informed in advance of any increase and in the unlikely event of a mistake, your bank will refund you immediately. You may cancel your debit instruction at any time.

If you pay UK income tax and complete a DEED of COVENANT, the RA can recover around 33p for each pound you pay at NO EXTRA COST TO YOU. The covenant is automatically cancelled if you cease to be a member of the Association.

Please tick if you wish to receive either :

A Direct Debiting instruction ▶
and/or a Deed of Covenant ▶

YES NO ☐ ☐

WHO SPEAKS FOR US ....?

When you set out for a country walk you are taking part in Britain's most popular outdoor recreation, with a quarter of the population keeping you company.

Love and appreciation of fine countryside runs deep in our national character, and more of us than ever before take a regular chance to escape into rural surroundings. Striking out over open country, exploring rural footpaths, literally millions have already discovered that you only *really* experience the countryside when you go on your own two feet.

So we *all* have a stake in the future of our countryside, and in our rights of access to it.

You may enjoy an idyllic day out. But there are ominous clouds over the landscape — threats which make it vitally important that millions of walkers and strollers have an effective voice in matters of country concern. The Ramblers' Association *is* that voice.

Take a walk with us, and see why the Ramblers are so important to you . . .

The footpath we follow is just one tiny part of a unique network of 135,000 miles of paths and ways in rural England and Wales. They are called rights of way because you walk them *as a right* — not because a landowner allows you to. But they are nowhere near as secure as you would expect.

Thousands of paths are blocked every year, most often by growing crops. A recent Ramblers' survey showed that 75% of paths crossing arable fields were difficult or sometimes just impossible to follow. Barbed wire, locked gates, even buildings turn up on paths to deny you your rights.

Every year, too, many hundreds of paths are swallowed up by new housing, roads, quarries and industry. Hundreds more are diverted from their traditional line — usually to a roundabout route which happens to suit the landowner.

The Ramblers believe that authorities should stop penny-pinching on public paths and allot them a budget which matches their recreational value today. We believe that peristent offenders should no longer get away with path blocking, and our own successful prosecutions show the way.

We are constantly on the alert. When people meet with path problems they report them to us and the Ramblers' footpath volunteers go to work. They take up the issues, put your case at public inquiries and try to get action wherever a path is in trouble. You owe your enjoyment of many a quiet country path to their unceasing efforts.

The landscape seems unchanging but look again! Unless we can turn the tide of destruction, our much-loved countryside patchwork of hedge and woodland will be unknown to future generations.

Many hedgerows have been settling their roots in the land for hundreds of years and are a wonderful wildlife haven. Yet today they are under threat. In 40 years we have ripped up over 100,000 miles of hedgerow, felled farmland trees, put downland under the plough and seen vast tracts of our 'green and pleasant land' ruthlessly stripped bare.

Elsewhere, grim lines of conifers march inexorably over open uplands, rapacious quarries claim more virgin land, and road planners cast covetous eyes on precious countryside wherever their invasion of noise and concrete will meet least resistance.

Green fields and quiet rural places cannot argue for their own survival — so who will speak for them? The Ramblers, of course. Recent campaigns aimed to save the hedgerows, stop forestry tax-evasion, curb the use of dangerous pesticides, and keep new roads out of outstanding landscapes like the New Forest.

Wherever our remaining natural beauty is under threat, the Ramblers will be there — researching the arguments, gathering the evidence, speaking up for countrygoers. We believe that losing this beauty would take something vital from all our lives — and that its value *must* be balanced against all the materialistic arguments. The issues are as grave as that.

◀ **JOIN THE RAMBLERS** . . . .

THE FUTURE OF WEALDWAY

As we have seen, Wealdway is never far from a multitude of pressures. In the past some of these have been major projects, some of a lesser nature. Nevertheless this means we have to keep constant vigil to monitor and maintain the route. Such work is worthwhile because Wealdway has now given pleasure to countless thousands of walkers. It has also contributed to a new awareness of how precious the countryside is for recreational use, among its many other purposes.

The future will be increasingly a balance of the dire needs of conservation and development. The Channel Tunnel Rail Link and the proposed second London orbital motorway are but two new dangers. Perhaps the most alarming proposal is a Strategic Route, the East-West trunk road, which would devastate the Wealdway in the Groombridge-Withyham valley.

We have to take the optimistic view that mature reason will prevail, to ensure that a priceless heritage does not become yet another bit of the environment ruined beyond repair!

Wealdway at some future date may become an 'Official' route, a responsibility of the Countryside Commission. But for the present, it remains truly established as a route of high repute in the care of Ramblers' Association members. They, in turn, depend on the goodwill and effort of individual ramblers; so if you are interested in offering your support, please turn to page 32 for further details.

AFTER YOUR WEALDWAY WALK

We hope you enjoyed your Wealdway walk and that you would like to explore more of Kent and Sussex. Perhaps also to meet and join with fellow enthusiasts. In the following pages information is provided for your help and guidance.

Beechy Toll. Wealdway between Hayesden and Bidborough (p.16) ▲

CONNECTING LONG DISTANCE WALKING ROUTES WITH WEALDWAY

Wealdway now links with seven other LD routes providing a variety of opportunities to extend a walking holiday. A popular choice is Wealdway to Eastbourne, then the South Downs Way to Winchester, a total of about 190 miles. Apart from the addresses below, guides are also stocked by the RA HQ.

*'Official Route' (Countryside Commission) The other routes are 'Unofficial' created by individuals/organisations or local authorities.

SAXON SHORE WAY
Length : 140 miles
Start : GRAVESEND · KENT
Finish : RYE · EAST SUSSEX

LINKS WITH WW AT GRAVESEND
Mr. C. Whittington
55 Chart Place
Gillingham ME8 0ID

LONDON COUNTRY WAY
Length : 205 miles
Circumnavigates
Greater London

LINKS WITH WW AT SOLE ST/TROTTISCLIFFE
Keith Chesterton
Guide to the London Country Way
A Constable Guide

NORTH DOWNS WAY*
Length : 145 miles
Start : DOVER · KENT
Finish : FARNHAM · SURREY

LINKS WITH WW AT TROTTISCLIFFE
Countryside Commission
Dower House, Cheltenham
Glos GL50 3RA

VANGUARD WAY
Length : 63 miles
Start : CROYDON · SURREY
Finish : SEAFORD · E. SUSSEX

LINKS WITH WW AT ASHDOWN FOREST/ BUXTED PARK/CHIDDINGLY
Vanguard Rambling Club
109 Selsdon Park Road, Croydon CR2 8JJ

SUSSEX BORDER PATH
Length : 200 miles
Start : EMSWORTH · HANTS
Finish : RYE · EAST SUSSEX

LINKS WITH WW AT WITHYHAM
Dr. B. Perkins
11 Old London Road, Brighton
East Sussex BN1 8ZR

GREENSAND WAY
Length : 145 miles
Start : HAZLEMERE · SURREY
Finish : HAMSTREET · Nr RYE

LINKS WITH WW AT WEST PECKHAM
SURREY SECTION (55 miles)
Public Rel. Unit, County Hall
Kingston-on-Thames KT1 2DN

WEST KENT/EAST KENT SECTIONS (2)
Mr. D. Stewart, 99 Woodside, Wigmore
Gillingham, Kent ME8 0PW

SOUTH DOWNS WAY *
Length : 108 miles
Start : EASTBOURNE
Finish : WINCHESTER

LINKS WITH WW AT EASTBOURNE
EASTBOURNE-BURITON (80 miles)
Countryside Commission
Cheltenham (see address NDW)

BURITON-WINCHESTER (28 miles)
Mr. H. Comber, 254 Victoria Drive
Eastbourne, East Sussex BN20 8QT

SELECTED BOOKS FOR YOUR FURTHER READING AND ANTICIPATION

KENT

VISITORS GUIDE TO KENT	Kev Renolds	Moorland 1985
PORTRAIT OF THE RIVER MEDWAY	Roger Penn	Robert Hale

SUSSEX

THE WILMINGTON GIANT	Rodney Castleden	Turnstone Press
VISITORS GUIDE TO SUSSEX	Jim Cleland	Moorland 1985
VIEW OF SUSSEX	Ben Darby	Robert Hale 1982
PORTRAIT OF SUSSEX	Cecile Woodford	Robert Hale 1984

GENERAL

THE COMPANION GUIDE TO KENT & SUSSEX	Keith Spence	Collins 1989
THE SOUTH EAST, DOWN & WEALD. KENT, SURREY & SUSSEX	John Talbot-White	Eyre Methuen 1977
JOURNEY THROUGHOUT THE WEALD	Ben Darby	Robert Hale 1986
THE JUTEISH FOREST	Kenneth Whitney	Athelon Press
PORTRAIT OF ASHDOWN FOREST	Roger Penn	Robert Hale 1984
IN THE WAKE OF THE HURRICANE NATIONAL EDITION	Bob Ogley	Froglets

▲ Arlington Church (p.27/28)

RAMBLERS' ASSOCIATION
Tel: 071 582 6878
See page 32

LONG DISTANCE WALKERS' ASSOCIATION
Wayfarers, 9 Tainters Brook, Uckfield
East Sussex TN22 1UQ

RA KENT AREA SECRETARY
Mr. B. Arguile, 42 Waldron Drive
Loose, Maidstone, Kent ME15 9TH

RA NORTH WEST KENT
Mr. C. Tottle, 13 Lancaster Close
Bromley, Kent BR2 0QF

RA TONBRIDGE & MALLING
Mr. B. F. Gregson, 87 Elmhurst Gardens
Tonbridge, Kent

RA TUNBRIDGE WELLS
Mr. M. Temple, Ploggs Hall East Barn
Whetstead, Tonbridge, Kent TN12 6SE

SOCIETY OF SUSSEX DOWNSMEN
93 Church Road, Hove
East Sussex BN3 2BA

SOUTH EAST ENGLAND TOURIST BOARD
1 Warwick Park, Tunbridge Wells
Kent TN2 5TA. Tel: 0892 40766

RA SUSSEX AREA SECRETARY
Mrs. P. C. Mills, 6 Gladstone Road
Burgess Hill, West Sussex RH15 0QQ

RA BEACHY HEAD
Mrs. A. Griggs, 55 Babylon Way
Eastbourne, East Sussex BN20 9DE

TUNBRIDGE WELLS CHA & HF RAMBLING CLUB
Miss C. McClare, 5 Guestwick
Tonbridge, Kent TN10 4HU

EASTBOURNE RAMBLING CLUB
Mr. G. N. Thompson, 65 Wrestwood Avenue
Eastbourne, East Sussex

THE COUNTRY CODE

- Use gates and stiles to cross fences, hedges and walls • Guard against all risks of fire
- Take special care on country roads • Help to keep all water clean • Fasten all gates
- Keep to public paths across farmland • Leave livestock, crops and machinery alone
- Enjoy the countryside and respect its life and work • Protect wildlife, plants and trees
- Keep dogs under control • Make no unnecessary noise • Take all your litter home